House of Fire

Additional praise for *House of Fire*:

"*House of Fire* is a book of naked, sharp-edged truth, a journey into and through immense darkness. Yet it is also a profound testament to our deeply human ability to heal and transform."

– Scott Edelstein, author, *Sex and the Spiritual Teacher*

"Truly, this is a story of love, courage, transformation and determination. Beautifully written. It really works well with the back and forth from present to past, and isn't that how we all live our lives, clearing the past so we can fully arrive in the present the Real life, having learned from what has come before?"

– Cindy Yasmine Libman, LICSW, LMFT, CAEH

"Out of the ashes of her harrowing childhood, Elizabeth di Grazia has crafted a tale of hope and renewal. In unsentimental and forthright prose, di Grazia shares how she managed to break the chains of childhood incest and create a loving family from scratch—not by erasing her past but by absorbing its hard lessons. Her resilience and determination shine through every page. This book shows it is possible not only to survive the unimaginable, but also to thrive in spite of it."

– Pamela Schmid, editor, *Sleet Magazine*

HOUSE OF FIRE

A story of love, courage, and transformation

By
ELIZABETH DI GRAZIA

NORTH STAR PRESS OF ST. CLOUD, INC.
St. Cloud, Minnesota

ISBN: 978-1-68201-028-0

First edition: March 2016

Printed in the United States of America.

Published by
North Star Press of St. Cloud, Inc.
P.O. Box 451
St. Cloud, MN 56302

northstarpress.com

To my family:
Jody, Antonio, and Crystel

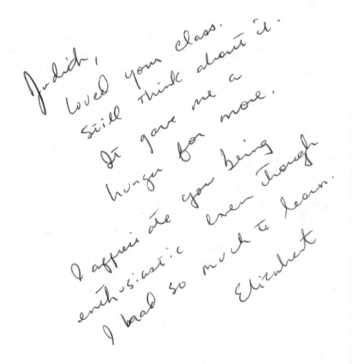

Judith,
Loved your class.
Still think about it.
It gave me a
hunger for more.
I appreciate you being
enthusiastic even though
I had so much to learn.

Elizabeth

Author's note

I've changed the names of my brothers and sisters, except my youngest brother, John. He needs to be seen; I want everyone to see him. This is my story. No one can say that it didn't happen.

Hope is the thing left to us in a bad time.
                                                    –Irish proverb

Mary Patricia Krantz	married	George Edward Smith
3/15/24–10/26/91	5/2/53	7/23/20–12/26/92
Simon		May 11, 1954
Patrick		April 12, 1955–December 19, 2012
David		July 6, 1956–April 29, 2015
Thomas		July 13, 1957
Ann		**September 26, 1958**
Mark		April 25, 1960
Michael		April 13, 1961
Paul		November 20, 1962
Catherine		June 20, 1964
Margaret		November 30, 1966
Patricia		July 31, 1968
John		November 14, 1969–May 29, 1999

PART
ONE

Part One

DRAGGING OUR LUGGAGE TO THE INTERNATIONAL AIRLINE counter, I shortened my stride to stay behind Jody. Her trim runner's body, a weather vane, was my directional. She was stressed. I could tell by the way she carried her five-foot, three-inch frame—taut spine and determined walk. I shortened my stride because I had to practice not being Jody's partner.

Morning passengers were checking flight information or moving quickly to their terminals. Conversation was a low hum, mixed with the shuffling of gray plastic tubs and the rustle of coats, jackets, and shoes being removed at security.

The dark blue trailing suitcase tipped over again. It was unwieldy, bulging with everything two babies would need for a stay in a hotel. Bracing the baggage with my foot, I yanked it upright. I was overdressed because I didn't like to be cold. I tugged at my layers, pulling them away from my clammy skin. Jody reached for one end of the large suitcase and helped me slide the baggage to the counter. She tucked her short brown hair behind her ears.

"You gals traveling to Guatemala to adopt?" asked the gate agent.

"Yes we are," we answered in unison.

My eyes burned. The airline attendant saw us as partners, both moms-to-be. I set down my backpack and busied myself in locating our passports, burying my glee. I hoped Jody didn't notice the inclusive language the attendant used. The previous night she had suggested we remove our matching rings. She was wound tighter than strands of cat hair in a grooming brush.

Jody would be the legal mother. She was adopting Antonio and Crystel, seven– and eight-month-olds. In Guatemala, it was illegal for same-sex couples to adopt. Even in 2003, there were efforts in at least sixteen U.S. states to establish laws requiring that children be adopted or fostered only by heterosexual couples and singles. The adopting mother could easily have been me. However, we gambled that Jody's job would be the most secure. A year earlier, when we started the adoption process, unemployment jumped to an eight-year high. If we chose wrong and the single parent was laid off and lost her income, we would lose our possibility of a family. For us to be successful in adopting, I had to agree to not exist on paper. This went against everything I believed in. I was now disposable, just like I was in my birth family. Wounds I carried from being unseen were again ripped open.

It wasn't that my mother never saw me. While in my twenties, I gave the eulogy for my maternal grandmother to a standing-room-only crowd in a Catholic church. After the service, my mother asked me for the tribute and had seventy-five copies made for the reception. Though surprised, I was happy. She was obviously proud of her daughter. She worked the room until her hands were empty.

It was déjà vu at my boyfriend's funeral. She called asking for the address to the funeral home. Again, I was taken aback.

I could not reconcile this mother who abandoned me in my childhood and teens with the mother who now, sometimes, wanted to be a part of my life. On this occasion, her attention unsettled me. I didn't know where to sit—with the boyfriend's mother, my parents, or friends? I had this extra problem to deal with. My dad, who was also there, didn't register in my mind. He was absent even when he was present. Mother made him come. She always made him show up for the things she didn't want to do alone. I could picture her shooing him to the sink to shave, the shaving cream left behind his ears, and the suit that he was now wearing that she would had laid out on the bed.

SUDDENLY, THE BOYFRIEND'S MOTHER, who wasn't much different from mine, put her henlike arms around me and pulled me to the front row, seating me next to her. I sobbed throughout the service for what wasn't and what could never be and for reasons that I didn't even know.

A couple years later, my mother was there at my college graduation. I was thirty years old. It took me thirteen years to cobble together tuition reimbursement, vocational rehabilitation grants, and money to walk onto the stage and receive my bachelor's degree. After the ceremony, she took me out for dinner. I was surprised she had even wanted to be a part of the celebration. My first thoughts were that I'd just receive my diploma in the mail and skip the hullabaloo until she inserted herself into my life and said that she wanted to come. Dad, silent and unseen, was with her. He never seemed to get his due. It was he who gave me a ring as a graduation present, which I would soon lose. I would never find it, though I

looked and looked. My dad was a chemical dependency counselor by then. The *Chippewa Herald-Telegram* had recently
written an article about him.

> Recovering alcoholic works for Alcohol, Drug Abuse
> Council: A counselor from the Division of Vocational
> Rehabilitation office says, "George can move into a fam-
> ily situation and immediately know the problems. He
> has an uncanny knack for communication. People relate
> to him quickly because of that. He is highly respected
> in the field. He is in homes and treatment centers all
> hours of the day. If you need something, call George."

I knew the man, my dad, who was depicted in the story. I
also knew the man who was scared, vulnerable, beaten down,
and who fondled my breasts. Dad was well liked, respected,
and generous. It was his family who struggled. His family who
treated him as if he was a nothing. Maybe we were just trying
to find him.

Next, I received a letter from my mother that said she was
making plans to visit me in Tonga, where I was stationed in
the Peace Corps. She would bring gifts for my homestay family. She never came. It could have been my anger that kept her
away. By then, I had her figured out. She showed up when I
made her look better. She wanted to take credit for who I was,
who I had become.

My eight brothers got the worst of it. She didn't pay them
any attention. If I was disposable, they were trash in the burn
barrel. Maybe it was because they didn't make anything of
themselves. In my early twenties, my Aunt Flora told me, "You
are a self-made woman."

The adoption agency knew Jody and I were partners. They cushioned my feelings, the unseen partner, by saying that they would write the home study report as a composite of us. Visiting our home, the social worker affirmed our relationship by using eye contact, including me in the discussion, and assuring us of a successful adoption. Still, I couldn't help my anger. When the home study report came for us to proofread, not existing on paper scalded me. For ten years, I worked so hard to heal, and being visible in the world was a large part of that. Now, to have these babies, I had to erase myself all over again. This time it was my doing. I wanted a family that much. By now, my mother was dead. I was happy that she was dead. My life was easier. Now, I was focusing on creating my own family. My dad was dead, too. Both, a pile of ashes in a box, buried side by side.

The home study said that Jody moved into her story-and-a-half-style house two years ago, in a safe, quiet neighborhood next to a school with a playground, softball field, hockey rink, and tennis courts. The house had three bedrooms, two bathrooms, a dining room, kitchen, a living room with a fireplace, a three-season porch, an exercise room, and another bedroom, laundry room, and storage in the basement. The report said the entire house was open, comfortable, attractively furnished, and reflected her interests and tastes. The fenced backyard was beautifully landscaped, with a swimming pool. It had plenty of room for children to play.

What the home study didn't state was that this was my home for eight years before I met Jody. It didn't say that at one point I had three renters to help with the mortgage during a period of unemployment. Jody and I refinanced the house when she moved in and she became a joint owner. Months later, even though it wasn't legal or recognized by the State of Minnesota, we married in the backyard.

"Passports, please?"

I pushed aside two paperbacks to reach the passports. I was the holder of important, irreplaceable papers. I had learned about Jody's propensity for misplacing items on our first vacation, a three-week backpacking trek in New Zealand. It became customary for us to hunt for her valuables by backtracking from one scenic location to the next. Before our holiday was over, she handed me her passport, her return flight ticket home, and her car and house keys. I loved that she had decided to travel overseas with me. I'd come up with the adventure and she'd agreed to accompany me, was thrilled, even. Toward the end of a trip, when I no longer had any money, she would treat me. Even from the very beginning, it was clear she wanted to be with me.

"Most people treat the stroller as a carry-on," the attendant said. "Then, they can make sure it reaches their destination."

I kept my gaze inside the backpack. I'd do anything to not respond. Unlike me, Jody usually processed information before she talked. I gained understanding as the words flowed. The more I talked, the more I knew. I wished people like her had taxi meters for eyeballs, indicating that they were thinking and they'd be responding soon. It would be my signal to remain silent. Instead, I lived in this not-knowing place. I had no idea where Jody was on the continuum of being verbal. It jarred her when I spoke too soon and she didn't have the length of time she needed for her thoughts.

"Okay," Jody said after a minute. "We'll bring it with us."

Burnt jet fuel and the smell of fresh coffee were in the air. My stomach was growling.

Jody took possession of the stroller, but later, as we sliced through the current of people, we heard, "Would the person who left a child's stroller at security please return to the area?"

Jody was gripping a carry-on in one hand and a backpack in the other.

I stopped mid-stride.

"I forgot," she argued. "They wouldn't let the stroller go through the scanner."

"Jeez, I hope we don't forget the babies someplace." I gripped my backpack tight, comforted by its bulk.

"Shsssh!" She took three quick steps back to security. "There it is, leaning against the wall!"

I shifted my pack to carry the full weight on my back and held out my hand. "Here, let me take it."

Her face was flushed. "No, I have it!"

She was juggling her bags and the umbrella stroller. Her right shoulder couldn't contain the weight of her carry-on. The bag slid to her elbow, causing her to lose her grip on the stroller. The stroller flopped to the ground.

"Let me help."

"No!" she said again. "I have it!"

She flung the carry-on strap over her neck, leaned, and grabbed the stroller's handle. The stroller wasn't worth much. It still had a sticker from a garage sale: five dollars.

It's not like losing a baby, I wanted to say. I now wondered if that was a possibility.

THE SUN WAS SETTING when the plane circled over Guatemala City. I studied volcano peaks out the window. There were thirty-three volcanoes in Guatemala, some very active, regularly covering the surrounding towns and villages in thick ash. Nineteen miles southwest of Guatemala City was Pacaya, an active complex volcano. Pacaya erupted violently in 1965, and had been erupting continuously since then. My babies were born here. I was born near unpredictable fire, as well.

Three other large volcanoes were masses on the horizon out the airplane window. One of them, Volcano de Fuego (Volcano of Fire), remained constantly active at a low level; steam and gas issued from its top daily. Once, in October of 1974, Fuego erupted. An ash cloud shot more than four miles high. Glowing avalanches moved down the slopes of the Volcano of Fire at thirty-five miles per hour. In 1974, I was fifteen years old. I lived far from here, but like the Guatemalans, I was running from fire.

I pressed my forehead against the cool glass of my seat window while the memory stalked me.

IT WAS MID-MORNING on our Wisconsin farm. Fifty dairy cows, milked hours ago, were grazing in the pasture. A nip still hung in the air, but I burned.

It was a breezy September morning. Warming my back against the trash barrel, the flames must have caught the synthetic lettering on my shirt. It wasn't even mine. It was a wrestling top, a brother stole from a rival school. When my mother found out that the athletic garb wasn't flame resistant she wanted to sue the school, but how was she going to explain how he got the shirt? I was surprised I had it on. I was risking a pounding, wearing his shirt. But if he stole it, it was anybody's, right?

The trash barrel had been moved to the front of the garage. The garage had been lined with beds for my brothers when our house burnt down. That was three years earlier. Today, we were burning rubbish from the yard, the basement, and the garage. Everything disappeared in the flames, a left-over shoe, sock, cardboard, wood, paper. Even clothes. Now the fire wanted me.

I ran. The fire followed. I fell to the grass, slapping at my shoulders, my back, my side. I screamed. Digging my teenage shoulders into the ground, I pitched back and forth, back and forth.

My ten-year-old sister screeched for our brother. "Mark! Ann's on fire!"

Flames reached for my hair. My hands slapping, slapping, always slapping, but heat scorched me everywhere. I was inside the fire. I struggled for the earth, using the grass, the dirt to snuff the fire that was burning me alive.

Mark finally reached me. He tore off what was left of my shirt, threw the burning scrap into the rusty trash barrel. Flames and black smoke swirled in the cylinder. I was naked from the waist up. I crossed my arms in front of me, hiding my breasts, and ran into the basement of our home.

Mother was in the basement putting clothes in the washer. "Get in the shower!"

I stood under the spray, my body shaking, shivering. I touched my hair. The ends were brittle. My back was a mouth-full of nerves, Pop Rocks, crackling, fizzing, and popping.

"All right, get out here."

She handed me a button-down, washed-out plaid shirt of Dad's. I smelled it, sniffing for cow shit. Did she get it from the rack or pick it out of the pile on the floor? I studied the mound of dirty clothes below my feet. Still doubtful, I swung the shirt on my back and quickly put my arms through the short sleeves. I was drowning in his shirt. Pinching the sides of the cloth, I held it away from my burnt skin so the fabric wouldn't touch me. I didn't want anything of my dad's touching me. Hunched over, trembling, I drew in short, quick breaths. I had a problem. I couldn't get out of my wet shorts without letting go of the shirt. If I let go of the shirt, it would touch my skin. Still, I couldn't help it. I quickly dropped my hands, pawed out of my pants, and left them in a puddle on the concrete floor. When the shirt touched my skin, it felt like hot grease jumping from a pan.

The three bedrooms in the basement were quiet. My younger brothers and sisters were scattered into hiding, afraid to be involved in the commotion. I wanted to find them and tell them that it would be all right. Instead, I walked upstairs to the kitchen. The smell of fried potatoes and onions permeated the house.

"George, goddamn it, why can't you take her!" I heard my mother yelling. "Jesus Christ, can't you see I'm busy cooking? Can't you do a goddamn thing? Why is it always me? You take her!" Mother stabbed at the insides of the cast-iron frying pan to loosen stuck potatoes.

My dad shook his head back and forth. His beefy face was drained of color. "I'm . . . I'm . . . not going to take her!"

"George, goddamn it! You drive her!"

I stood for a moment staring. She wanted Dad, the Nothing, to take me to the doctor? My back was burnt to shit. I hadn't stopped shaking. "Forget it!" I yelled from the doorway, my hand already on the knob. "I'll fucking walk!" My voice stopped them. It was four miles to the doctor's office.

"You son of a bitch!" Mother said to Dad, throwing the metal spatula at him. "Call the doctor. Tell him to wait."

Mother and I didn't speak during the five-minute drive into town. Leaning forward in the car, I grabbed at the shirt to fan it away from my skin. My attempts were futile. A whistling sound came in and out between my clenched teeth. I tasted smoke. My heart was pounding. Would the doctor ask me about the baby? Is that why Mother didn't want to take me? Mother signaled a right turn at the Ellsworth East End Bank. There were two doctors in our town of three thousand: the Catholic doctor, Dr. Klaas, and the other one, Dr. Jonas. Dr. Klaas had his office on the east end of town and Dr. Jonas on the west end. That's how the town was divided: Catholic and other. Dr. Klaas and his family attended High Mass on Sundays. They sat in the third pew from the front. My brothers were altar boys, my mother a lector, my father converted.

The last time I saw Dr. Klaas as a patient was a year earlier. I was fourteen. I went in with severe stomach pains. Dr. Klaas diagnosed my pregnancy. But it was Dr. Jonas, the doctor on the other side of town, who referred my parents to an abortion clinic in the Twin Cities.

Even though it was just after noon on Saturday, and the sign in the window said the office was closed, a nurse met us at the door and motioned us in. "Dr. Klaas will examine you in the first room."

"Take your shirt off," Dr. Klaas said gently. "Lay down."

After giving me a shot in the butt, he reached for the tweezers. Moving to my back, he began pulling off skin, strip by strip. The smell of charred skin and singed hairs filled the room. I was horror-struck that the doctor was peeling me. A potato is peeled. I spasmed on the white paper.

"How did this happen?"

I mumbled into the table, "trash barrel . . . warming back . . . caught . . . on fire."

Did he believe me? Did he believe me when I told him it wasn't my brothers who got me pregnant? I smelled more scorched skin. The shot took care of any pain. The doctor found places that I didn't know were burned—fingers, palms, parts of my arm. Still flat on the table, I turned my hand over, studying my fat fingers. I was surprised at the large blisters, already filling with fluid. I was a volcano spilling lava everywhere.

"You're going to have to go to the hospital in Red Wing," he said. "I'll treat you there."

GUATEMALA'S LA AURORA International Airport appeared below. Jody leaned across me to peer out the small window. Together, we took in the panorama of mountains circled by green, hilly foliage. It was a steep decline onto a narrow runway. I waited for the sudden dive and drop with quick and shallow breaths. The landing was smooth.

After checking into our hotel, we walked in step to the elevator. Both of us were eager to be in the room where our family would be born.

Our suite was huge—a sitting room with sofa and overstuffed chair, small refrigerator, desk, sleeping area with two queen-size beds, two cribs, and a television. A knock stopped our movements. I turned to open the door and suddenly paused. The mother would open the door, not the friend, not the sister, certainly not the partner. "Jody, answer the door," I whispered urgently. I backed away, providing her space to step in front of me.

"Shssh. I am."

Jody reached for the knob. I gawked over her shoulder, my chest lightly touching her back. The doorway was filled with a short, Guatemalan woman wearing a blush of reddish hues, holding a grinning baby boy. She held the baby upright, his feet pedaling furiously.

He was beautiful.

I had never seen anyone so beautiful. His captivating smile drew me. His grin showed four top and two bottom teeth. Charm radiated from his body and he had an effervescent glow about him; his dark eyes danced, beckoning us closer. I'd remember this forever—his smile, his teeth, his teeth! He had teeth!

Jody peered past Antonio. "Where's Crystel?"

"We'll bring her tomorrow," a man standing behind the woman said. The man was the adoption lawyer.

The woman passed Antonio to Jody. She and the baby sat on the sofa. Magnetized by Antonio, I offered a seat to the woman and man with a flash of my hands and sat next to Jody. Jody slowly and carefully handed Antonio to me while she fumbled for our list of questions. She patted her front pockets. Ogling Antonio, I nodded in the direction of the television. "The list is over there."

My stomach tensed. Would a friend kiss the baby or was that too intimate? I shrugged. Kissing Antonio's black hair, I permitted him to pull my fingers to his mouth. "Ouch! The little bugger bit me!" Blue marks were on my finger. My first parenting lesson: Don't let a baby teethe on you. There was laughter. Antonio laughed the most.

Jody asked about feeding times, formula, sleeping habits, what time in the morning we had to arrive at the embassy to do the paperwork, and when she would get the chance to meet her daughter. We said our goodbyes.

For the next hour, Antonio's jabbering filled the room. Finally, we placed him in his crib, where he immediately fell asleep. Night passed quietly with the eight-month-old, except for the rustling of the sheets when we left our bed to check on him. Bending low, we listened for his breath. We had yet to hear him whimper.

The next morning, I asked Jody if there was anything wrong with Antonio.

Jody spread the patchwork-print quilt over the bed and centered it so it hung evenly. She left the folded-down sheet and blanket exposed at the top, but covered their bottom edges.

"The adoption agency said to expect a developmentally delayed baby. Did you see him pulling himself up just by grasping the bedspread?" I added.

She topped the bed off with a throw. "He's wonderful. He's ours."

"Look at him sleeping in his crib. His body is moving. See his leg kicking?"

"He's ours." She gave the pillow a slap.

Morning was hurried when Antonio woke. He kept us busy as we spent time holding him down to change his diaper, bathe him, and put on his clothes. He wiggled from our laps, waving his arms when we tried to feed him. Jody slipped on a dress for the embassy visit.

Brushing her hair, her hand stopped in midair. "Oh no, we're wearing our matching heart necklaces."

Sitting on the bed entertaining Antonio with a rattle, I fingered the gold chain around my neck and glanced at the diamond nestled inside the heart. "I'll take mine off."

"Oh, forget it. Let's leave them on." She turned back to the mirror.

Morning light filtered through the sheer curtain blinds.

"No. No. I'll take mine off," I said, reaching for the clasp.

"You know, you called me 'hon' last night when they were here. I lifted your hand off my thigh. I hope no one noticed."

"Oh, oh." I had a life-long struggle with intimacy. I rarely held Jody's hand. In bed or on the couch, I didn't lie down next to her and gaze into her eyes. She would love it if I did. Our fear of being found out had brought into light the affection that I did show. Even though I was concerned about this relapse, a sigh escaped my lungs, a deep, gratifying sigh. I was evolving. Growing up, my family didn't show affection. There were no hugs and no terms of endearments and no raising of the eyebrows with a hint of a smile. Oddly, we did scratch feet. Watching television, it was common for me to recline and scratch a brother's foot while he scratched mine.

During my early twenties, in a therapy session with my mother, I imagined she and I sitting on the floor and her enveloping me in her arms. I wondered if I dared ask her to hold me. Could I actually get what I never got? Could this be a do-over? I just couldn't do it. The thought of her cradling me took my breath away. I could not be that vulnerable.

Once, when I was ten, I woke up and she was sitting next to my bed in a chair reading a book. It was late afternoon and I had been running a high temperature. She said she was waiting for my fever to break. It was so quiet, so peaceful. I jumped and ran out of the house to look for my siblings. Though it felt nice to have her present, I was much more comfortable with my siblings.

In the lobby, waiting for the adoption lawyer, Jody cradled Antonio in her arms. I sat several inches from her. I promised myself not to call her "hon." I promised not to touch her. I promised myself only to be her friend.

The lawyer was holding a bundle to his chest when he arrived at the hotel.

Jody took her eyes off Antonio. "Is that Crystel?"

"Yes, it is. I picked her up at her foster mother's home," he said.

"It's her?" I asked incredulously. I never really believed that it could happen, that two people could actually create the family they so much wanted. Everything about this was a dream, another lifetime. I should have been dead, and would have been dead if I hadn't gotten out. Dead like my brother John was dead. Instead, I was being handed a bundle of life.

The lawyer passed the baby to me since Jody's arms were full. We had wanted to adopt both babies at the same time, but because they came from different mothers, the paperwork moved slower for Crystel. We'd have to come back to Guatemala for her, hopefully soon. But, for now, I was happy that we were adopting both infants. Jody and I yearned to be mothers. Each of us would have a baby to tend, a baby to hold. There wouldn't be any waiting until the other mother had her fill. When I lifted the blanket, my new daughter's eyes were closed. Her dark hair was thin around her oval face. Her tiny form didn't move. Suddenly, I remembered that I was not the mother. "Would you like to hold Crystel?"

We carefully shuttled babies.

On the ride to the embassy, Jody talked in such a quiet voice that I had trouble hearing her.

"Crystel's eyes haven't focused all morning. She's either sleeping or staring."

"Should we be concerned about her developmentally?" At this point, we could still choose not to adopt Crystel.

"I don't know. Let's wait and see."

Jody adjusted the blanket around Crystel. The movement caused the baby's eyes to open. She had wide, dark eyes. I watched her blink, and then she closed her eyes again.

After the embassy visit, I left our room to go to the hotel gift shop. I bought a Guatemalan blanket, dolls, drum, and oversized purse, which we would use for a diaper bag. When I returned, Crystel and Antonio were napping in their cribs.

"How did things go?" I asked.

Jody turned toward me. "I have a confession to make."

I leaned forward, tilted my head. I liked that about Jody. We didn't have secrets. Growing up in my family, if you weren't home you didn't know what was going on. And you'd never find out. One time I came home and Thomas was in the hospital getting a skin graft. He had gotten some part of his body caught in a piece of farm equipment. To this day, I don't know what happened because I wasn't there. Much smaller things happened than this, but it was a constant. For example, Mother gave me a lamb to raise when I was nine. We kept it in the house. I woke one morning and Lambkin was gone. She said that the lamb choked on a telephone cord. That just didn't seem right. When I left for college, I never learned what happened to my dog, Butch. There were so many stories. I wondered if my mother took the dog out in the field and shot it. I trusted my siblings more than I trusted my parents, but even then, you sometimes just didn't know what really happened because you weren't there.

"Um. Antonio, er . . ." Jody paused. "Fell off the bed while you were gone."

I raised my eyebrows. "Really?" I turned and hid my smile. Earlier, Jody had admonished me for placing Antonio on the back of the couch, letting him plummet into my arms. Antonio laughed deliriously and I was intoxicated with the sound. Though Jody frowned, I did it again and again.

Walking the length of the room, I peeked into the crib and took stock of the sleeping boy. My boy. Drool leaked out the corner of his mouth, creating a wet half-moon on the stiff white crib sheet. I studied his long dark eyelashes, his brown skin, and his black hair. I reached to feel its coarseness. His eyelids flickered. He pulled himself up to his knees, curling into himself. I had originally wanted to adopt from Russia. The children were white, had blue eyes, and looked like me. I figured they would only have one strike against them, two mothers. I also feared my capacity to love someone who looked different from me. I didn't have to worry. Antonio was completely my son.

Jody continued with a rush of words. "I . . . I . . . placed him in the middle of the bed . . . and . . . and ran into the bathroom for a quick second. The next thing I heard was this thud and . . . and . . . he was crying." She fidgeted with a pile of clean baby clothes. Stacking and restacking tiny onesies. "He's okay. He was just scared."

I scanned the queen-sized bed, the height, imagined Antonio tumbling. I was glad it wasn't me. "How's Crystel been?"

"Sleeping the whole time. She still hasn't taken her bottle."

I shook my head. "When you go back to the embassy, maybe you could ask her foster mother if this is normal." I sucked in a quick breath. "When are you going?" This would be my first time alone with two babies. "You're not going to stop any place on the way, are you? You'll be right back?"

"I'll only be gone for about two hours." She placed the onesies in a dresser. "I could take a baby with me."

"No, no. I'll be fine." I reached for a bottle of water out of the tiny refrigerator.

Rain sprinkled the window. Outside, people dashed from hotel to cab, hotel to restaurant, hotel to street. The room was too cool. The babies weren't accustomed to air conditioning. I adjusted the thermostat. I turned on the television and flipped channels. The two infants, each lying on their tummies on the queen-sized bed, lifted their heads. *Telletubbies* was playing. I made my acquaintance with Tinky-Winky, Dipsy, Laa-Laa, and Po. There was so much that I didn't know about parenting.

Antonio was excited, flailing his arms and kicking his feet. I stood him on the floor to keep his sister from being hit. He hung onto the bedspread with tight little fists. Crystel, lying on her tummy, kept her head raised, and bobbed up and down. She pushed her arms out as if she was flying. Mesmerized, she continued to stare at the television, her eyes tracking the movements of the four multi-colored toddlers. Picking up a soft blue baby blanket, I spread it on the bed and laid Antonio on it. I unsnapped his Beatrix Potter infant creeper and contemplated Elmo on the face of his diaper. Not long ago, my younger sister had teased me for putting a diaper on her daughter backwards. Before that, the last time I had changed a diaper (cloth and safety pins) was probably thirty-five years ago when she was a baby.

I held off before gripping the tape and undoing Antonio's diaper. I imagined my hands as my mother's. I shuddered. I didn't know until that moment how afraid I was of becoming my mother. I was afraid that incest was ingrained in a person, passed down the lineage. Tugging the tape, I unhinged the diaper, wiped him with a baby cloth and slid the diaper from underneath his butt. After dressing Antonio, I moved him to the headboard, climbed in next to him, and leaned my back against the stack of fluffy white pillows.

IT ALREADY SEEMED LIKE hours since Jody had left. I tapped my watch. Ten minutes. I propped Crystel against the pillows on the big bed. Her eyes had a twinkle. She moved her hands to her side, as if hitching up her yellow ducky outfit. When she smiled, she touched the roof of her mouth with her tongue. She didn't have any teeth.

Two hours passed. There was light knocking and Jody walked in.

"How did your trip go?" I asked, relieved.

"I have Antonio's passport and the documents that we need to leave the country. The foster mother is going to come for Crystel tonight about eight. She said that babies don't drink when they're in a new situation and that we shouldn't worry about her."

"But . . . but . . . Jody, she's hardly eaten, either."

Jody shrugged. "She said not to worry about it. When Crystel gets hungry, she'll eat." She set down a bag of groceries. "Maybe I'll go to the hotel nursery this afternoon and ask for ideas." Straightening the bottles on the counter, she made room for jars of baby food.

I dug in the grocery bag. "How did you know what to buy?" I picked up a jar. "Everything is in Spanish."

"I could make out some of the words and I looked at the color of the food." She set prepared and dry baby food on one side of the vanity, milk formula on the other.

Jody had listened to Spanish tapes for months. She worked hard to be a good mother and be ready for the infants. I just relied on the fact that I had mothered eleven siblings. I thought that would be enough.

"You always had enough to eat," my dad said.

"No one died," my mother said.

We waited for Crystel's foster mother to pick her up. Antonio fell asleep early and when Jody put him to bed, Crystel started crying.

"She's probably starved," I said. "Won't she die from dehydration if she doesn't drink something?" Tightness built in my chest.

Jody stood. "Her foster mother is an hour late. I'm going to take her for a walk. Maybe I can calm her."

She left, clutching the sobbing baby against her breast.

I suddenly wished Crystel's foster mother would arrive. Take her. *She's my daughter, we're going to keep her,* I told myself. But I was tired of her crying. I'd have plenty of time to be her mom when she came home with us.

Our hotel room was in disarray. I walked around, picked up waste, and placed it in the trashcan. I opened the suitcase, packed all the foodstuff we wouldn't need.

I opened our door and listened. Crystel's bawling floated down the hall from the nursery. I told myself a supportive partner would check in with her spouse. I had to learn how to be a loving partner. On occasion, I left "I love you" notes next to Jody's computer. I looked in on Antonio. He was sleeping.

I braced our door open, then walked quickly to the nursery. The room was empty except for Jody and Crystel.

"Do you want to take turns?" I offered.

Jody stood with Crystel and positioned her back to me. "No."

I wanted to say, "It's not your fault that she can't be soothed," but I was afraid Jody would be angry with me. Her greatest fear was that no matter how hard she tried, she wouldn't be a good mom. Just like she thought she was not a good-enough daughter, sister, and employee, maybe even partner. All I said was "Okay," and disappeared back to our suite. After picking up toys scattered around the floor, I wiped down the vanity. I checked on Antonio again, and then returned to the nursery.

"She still won't quit crying, huh?"

"I can't get her to stop." Tears broke free from Jody's eyes and she made a desperate sound in her throat.

"Here, let me take her. You take a break."

Sniffling, Jody handed Crystel over and left.

At six months old, Crystel weighed only ten pounds. Holding her with one arm, I bounced the crying infant up and down on my chest. I turned off the lights. Shadows jumped on the walls from streetlights shining through the hotel window. I closed the drape, transforming the room into a cave, hoping it would calm her. Babies liked the safety of the dark. I thought about the son I gave up for adoption in 1975. I was seventeen and pregnant again, for the second time, by one of my four older brothers. The maternity ward nurse had asked if I wanted to hold the newborn. I pictured him in my arms, me cradling him, squeezing him tight, like I was holding Crystel now. Though I had been sexually abused by my brothers for years, I kept my mouth shut all those years to protect my younger siblings from the same abuse, I couldn't hold my baby. I knew I wouldn't be able to let him go if I did.

I touched Crystel's tears. Did my son cry for me? I pulled Crystel closer. My tears wet her thin black hair, making it glisten in the weak light that slipped underneath the door.

"I'm sorry your mother is giving you away," I whispered to her. "I know what it's like not to be wanted." My chest began to heave, and my voice cracked. "I know that your mom wouldn't have given you away if she didn't have to."

I walked the long room, filled with weeping.

"I promise to take care of you, make sure that you know that you're wanted, loved." Words were stuck in my throat. "But I need your help. You have to eat, Crystel. You have to eat or you're . . . you're going to die."

I brought my daughter closer and squeezed her tight. My weeping matched hers. We sobbed together.

Shifting her tiny form, I placed my cheek on hers. Our moist skin touched. Her crying softened, than stopped. She curled into my neck. Tiny sucking noises came from her lips. I cradled her and realized that I never wanted to let her go.

IN GUATEMALA, FOR THREE DAYS Antonio was gregarious and flirty. His weeping started in the airport waiting area. I was afraid that he knew what was happening, that we were taking him from his birth country, his home, and his people. A Guatemalan man asked to hold him in order to comfort him. Antonio nuzzled into this man's shoulder and his crying stopped. *Good, he likes men.* I tucked this find away. Jody and

I were vigilant for clues to who Antonio was and what made him laugh, cry, and how to comfort him. Antonio must have found solace in this man's smell, the size of his hands, the roughness of his palms.

I smelled fried chicken. To my left, a Guatemalan woman had a carry-on filled with Pollo Campero. I looked around at the others standing and sitting in the small, crowded airport lounge. Many had the familiar yellow-and-white bags bulging with boxes of fried chicken piled atop their suitcases and sitting in their laps.

Guatemalan voices mingled with music. The man fussed to Antonio. I wondered what he was saying. I wondered what he must think of us.

ANTONIO'S COMING-HOME DAY was my mother's birthday. She had been dead for twelve years. I knew that it was her birthday because it was my job to know. My mother was overwhelmed with remembering important dates for all of her kids, twelve children in sixteen years. I was the one to remind her.

One year, my younger teenage brother, Mark, said to me, "Don't remind Mom that it's my birthday."

I was born between Thomas and Mark. Number five. First girl in the middle of seven boys. One of four girls.

Like all of us, Mark hoped our mother would remember.

"Are you sure? I wouldn't do that if I were you," I said, biting my lip. "She won't like that." Really, what I was worried about was Mark finding out the truth. I never dared not remind my mother that it was my birthday. I didn't want to know that she wouldn't remember. To me, that was proof that I was disposable. I tried to protect my siblings from the knowledge that all of us were throwaways. I was in awe of my brother, that he dared learn the truth.

Mark waited all day, too long, until there was no time to right the wrong. He finally brought it up to her at bedtime.

"Well, goddamn it," she said, glaring at me. She threw her book down.

And yet, there were times when Mother and Dad would take the birthday child to a local fishfry. David and Thomas would go together because their birthdays were one year and one week apart. On my birthday, I was able to invite a friend. This made the outing even more special. My father would stuff his suit pockets with crackers of different shapes and sizes. He'd pile them on the kitchen table for the kids who didn't come. Hands snatched the wafers from the tabletop.

ABOARD THE PLANE, I snuck a glance at the other passengers. Most were Guatemalan. Everybody could tell that Antonio wasn't our baby. He was brown and we were white. He was crying again. I wanted to hide. Any moment, I expected gun-wielding police officers to walk up the aisle, rip Antonio from our arms, and haul us out of the plane for stealing the infant, even though his adoption was legal. His wails shook his tiny body. The flight attendant stopped at our seats.

"Do you have any children's Tylenol?" she asked.

We nodded. Jody was holding tight to Antonio, his tears wetting her shirt.

"We already gave him some," she said with a tremble in her voice.

I avoided looking at Jody. If our eyes met, I'd start crying, too.

"If you don't mind, I'll walk with him," the flight attendant said. "Sometimes that helps."

Jody pushed Antonio into her arms. We heard his cries as she walked back and forth, securing the overhead luggage compartments.

That's our baby, the one who won't stop crying, I wanted to yell in defeat. There were no other infants on the plane. I wracked my brain, thinking of what we could do to console him. At the last possible moment, when it was time for the plane to be wheeled from the tarmac, the flight attendant brought Antonio, still sobbing, to us.

"Here, I'll take him," I said.

What do Guatemalan mothers do for a crying baby? What does any mother do?

One day, while I was in middle school, Mother laid baby Johnny on top of the clothes dryer. Maybe she thought the warm vibrations and humming white noise would soothe him and put him to sleep. She busied herself with house chores. He started crying. Finally, she picked him up. The back of his head was burnt. For years, no hair grew there. He had a bald spot the size of a silver dollar. She told us that she felt bad, that she didn't think the dryer got that hot. I put my hand on top of the dryer, feeling its heat. How long was he crying?

I thought back to the Guatemalans on the street walking with their infants strapped to their back or in a front sling. In spite of the warm sticky heat, babies were covered with blankets. I never saw their faces. I threw Antonio's fleece blanket over his head, shielding him from light and noise. He calmed, sniveling on my cheek. Are mothers supposed to know these things? Sweat from Antonio's head dribbled down my neck. I itched, but I dared not move. He had fallen into a restless slumber, his leg kicking the air. I was not accustomed to such a busy baby. Antonio's arms, legs, body, and head always were in motion. Is this because he was a boy? I was raised with eight brothers. Wouldn't this be familiar to me, as familiar as breathing?

Antonio's fleece blanket was soft and plush, with colorful satin-looped ribbon tags. I rubbed a tag between my fingers. My breaths became deeper. I closed my eyes.

During the flight, Jody jotted down notes about where to go in the airport, how to catch the tram, which line to stand in, picturing herself navigating the way alone with our daughter. She would be returning for Crystel as soon as we received the call.

I elbowed her lightly. "Did you write down not to forget the baby?"

Jody lowered her eyes at me.

Our life was so serious.

Aunt Kathy and Uncle Marty would be meeting us at the St. Paul/Minneapolis airport. Prior to Antonio and Crystel coming home, Jody and I created an extended family for the children, eight non-blood-related aunts and uncles. These men and women, straight and gay, single and married, were bonded to us by choice. They agreed to be significant in the children's lives, celebrating birthdays and holidays and visiting on a regular basis. Though I had eleven siblings, I'd never leave Antonio and Crystel alone with them. My greatest want was for my children to grow up without abuse. I wanted to witness what that looked like and I wanted that for them.

Kathy and Marty greeted us with hugs in the arrival area. Kathy took Antonio from Jody and cradled the tired eight-month-old. She looked at Antonio with a twinkle in her eyes and laughed loudly.

Passengers who had been on our plane had already swept by us. I had an ear tuned to the public address system announcing our baggage carousel.

Not long before, my Baptist sister, Catherine, told me that Jesus Christ was her savior and he was saving her and her family from the likes of Jody and me. I told her over and over that Jody and I were good people. Now that Jody and I had children, I was guarding them from the likes of her—people who may not protect my children from harm, people who place family loyalty above all else.

Kathy lovingly snuggled Antonio.

I tapped Jody's arm to get her attention. "Carousel four."

WALKING INTO OUR HOME, I caught sight of the feast spread out on our dining room table: baked original and spicy chicken wings, deviled eggs, Chinese salad, vegetables, and a fruit bowl. I brushed my tears away. Antonio crawled his way around the room. Aunts and uncles reached out to stroke his hair, his arm, his back. He was not frightened by the gentleness of their touches.

I sat on the floor, stretched, crossed my legs, and leaned back against the couch. I imagined Antonio and Crystel crawling over the legs of these aunts and uncles. Getting horsey-back rides, sitting on their laps and being cuddled. My eyes got teary again. Just what I wanted myself growing up and never got. I was determined to parent differently from how I was raised. I wanted to experience what love and attention could do for a child. Jody and I were alike in this way. She'd do whatever she needed to, to be a good mother.

After a couple of hours, Jody and I said goodbye to our guests. I set Antonio in his crib. He gripped the slats with both hands, pulled himself up, and reached for the bright balloon floating above him. He pulled the balloon string to his mouth. "Welcome Home," surrounded by a rainbow of stars.

Within three weeks, we received a call saying Crystel's paperwork had cleared the Guatemalan courts and she could come home. Jody boarded the flight for Guatemala.

MY FIRST NIGHT ALONE with Antonio was the worst. He would not sleep. He cried all the time. It was early April in Minnesota, blustery and cold. Frozen snow still packed our lawn. The weight of wanting to be a good mom pushed at me the same way the wind threw itself at our home. I thought caring for Antonio would be easy. I knew advice like, "don't hit, don't yell, and don't hurt," but even though I mothered my younger siblings, in the past few weeks I had come to realize that there was a lot more.

EVEN AS A FIVE-YEAR-OLD, I showed mothering traits. Playing with my brother, Mark, who was four, on a stationary steel plow, jumping from frame to runner, to shin, to trash board, he fell and couldn't get up. Older siblings ran to the house to tell Mom. I wanted to follow, be there with them in the excitement of the telling, the attention it would garner from our mother.

"Don't go," he said in a wee voice. "Stay with me."

He looked so helpless on the ground. Still, I wanted to catch up to my four brothers. A flock of sparrows suddenly flew up from the plowed field. I looked again at him and I couldn't leave. I tried to pick Mark up and carry him, but he was too heavy. I didn't know it then, but his leg was broken. With me walking and him crawling, we made our way across the large yard. It was eerily quiet and lonely with just the rustling of grass.

By the time I was sixteen, I was a full-time mother to my siblings.

During the school year, whenever my seven brothers wanted to skip school, they would come to me for a note. Practicing my dad's signature, I carefully scrawled "Geo E. Smith." He only used the first three letters for his first name— a lopsided pregnant "G" that bent toward the "e," followed by the "o" that looked as if it was running away. His middle initial "E" straightened at the top, got tired, and fell to a slant by the time it was done. I couldn't forget the period following the initial because he used it to prop up the "E." "Smith" was written in a hurry, as if he had no use for it.

My eighth brother, Johnny, was my little boy. He was the twelfth child in our family, the last one, the baby. My sisters were my little girls. They called me Mom.

"Mom!" Johnny yelled. He was five. His short legs tripped up the three cement steps into the house. He called again for me. I winced, knowing our mother was within earshot. I never corrected my siblings when they called me Mom, but it bothered me when they said it around Mother because if I was their mom, then who was she?

"What, Johnny?" I said.

Mother was sitting on the porch with *Reader's Digest*. She read large, thick books when I was little, moved to *Reader's Digest Condensed Books* in my teens, and would end her life with Harlequin romances. They'd wait for her—these pencil-thin romances. Hundreds of them. A shot of morphine anytime she wanted.

I glanced at my mother. She hadn't taken her eyes off her book.

"A bee stung me," Johnny cried. He jabbed, pointing to his arm.

"Come here." Opening the freezer, I grabbed an ice cube. I pulled him into my lap and held the ice on the hot red pinpoint. Water dripped between my fingers, down his scrawny dirty chicken wing of an arm.

"Better?"

"Yeah," he said, wiping his eyes and nose with the back of his other arm.

Three years later, when I was nineteen years old, I would have to leave Johnny to our mother. By then, it was him or me. I knew I would die if I stayed. God, I wish I could have taken him with me. But, I couldn't. I had no means to care for him. I had to save myself.

WHILE JODY WAS in Guatemala, there was no comforting Antonio. I took him out of the crib. I laid on my bed, held him on my chest. All I wanted was sleep. He whimpered. He sobbed. I moved him back to his crib.

"What do you want?" I asked. "What's wrong?"

I started to shake him. Then I realized it and was horrified. I quickly laid him on the hardwood floor. I picked him up and put him on the changing table. His eyes were glazed from tiredness. He wanted sleep, too. I held him tightly. Told him he was safe.

He was a bundle, a snail swaddled in soft blue flannel. He curled into my chest. We rocked. A homemade quilt was folded at the edge of the crib, its outline visible through the slats. Against one wall the silhouettes of unopened infant toys were propped on white shelving. Bobbing against the ceiling was Antonio's welcome balloon. I searched for his face. He was burrowed beneath the blanket. Perspiration running down my neck and under my shirt felt like spiders crawling across my skin. Antonio liked this moist incubator we had created. The only sounds were his short, rapid breaths.

In the darkness, the form nuzzling me became the baby I had at seventeen. I thought of him now, his adopted mother somewhere, how she must have felt rocking the baby that she wanted so much. I embraced my baby that someone else mothered, was mothering still. I pulled him tight as tears slid down my face.

Bending forward, I stood and lifted my baby and Antonio over the railing and into the crib. I didn't know that I was bringing home my baby when I boarded the plane in Guatemala City. Would Antonio have to compete with shadows he knew nothing about?

The phone rang. It was Jody. Her voice was light and happy, excitedly telling me all her news. Crystel was showing signs that she was interested in being fed, elongating her baby-bird neck, and reaching for the formula that dripped into her mouth . . . she cut the nipple on her bottle to allow the milky substance to trickle down her throat . . . she was wearing Crystel as if she were a bib in her Baby Bjorn front carrier . . . her body warmth comforted our daughter and Crystel was content to nest in the softness . . . her fear of traveling home was less . . . Crystel wasn't showing any signs of that "crying that won't stop."

I paced our kitchen floor, squeezed the phone to my ear. "Jody? Antonio is crying all the time." I suddenly resented that my partner was having the best of motherhood.

"Does he need to be seen by the—"

"I can't take him to the doctor." My voice was angry. "I'm not the adopting mother." I ground out the next sentence word by word as if it was her fault. "Antonio. And. I. Don't. Even. Have. The. Same. Last. Name."

Jody was silent.

I glared out our frosted kitchen window. Our backyard was a frozen sheet of ice. In Minnesota, in the winter, having a swimming pool was useless.

The fact was, I could take Antonio to the emergency room and demand that he be examined, but I didn't have the strength to respond to the questions that were sure to come. "What is your relationship to this baby? Do you have insurance? Where is his insurance card?" And the question that scared me the most: "Who is his mother, where is she?" I was truly afraid Antonio could be taken away from me. I already had one baby taken away.

"I'll be home tomorrow night," Jody said. "We'll take him in right away."

I didn't have a single sheet of paper anywhere in the world that said Antonio was my son. I was invisible, a fake, and a fraud. I had never been so stripped of rights except as a child in my own home. I had to keep Antonio hidden until his real mother came.

IN MY FAMILY, a child didn't go to the doctor unless it meant stitches, a broken limb, or a burnt back.

"Your psoriasis got burnt off your back in the fire," Dr. Klaas said.

"Oh, so that's what we have to do to get rid of them," my mother said with a laugh. "Burn them."

The scaly red patches had covered my legs, arms, stomach, and back since I was eight years old. Psoriasis was why my brothers called me "Scab."

In the hospital admittance area, we were two strangers, my mother and I. We sat diagonally across from each other, an end table separating us. She didn't know how to hold my hand, how to lean down and hug me. I didn't know how to talk to her. I had taken to snarling, twisting my left lip up. If she said anything, I might snap at her. It was safer for both of us not to talk. She picked up the most recent *Reader's Digest*. Without moving my head, I let my eyes float across the room. This wasn't the first time I had been on fire. At four, my blanket caught on fire because I was standing too close to the pot-belly stove. A year later, when I was five, I burnt my belly against a space heater. For months, I picked scabs off my tummy and stuck them in my mouth. Seemed like I was always trying to warm my insides.

The first night in the hospital, I slept on my back. I didn't feel any pain. The doctor gave me the strongest painkiller he had.

In the morning, after the nurse pulled off dead skin, she spread a white, creamy salve on my back. The pain started about the time she was done wrapping me in a long, wide bandage. For most of an hour, I sobbed. I stuffed my head in the white, stiff pillow to muffle my crying. My crying startled me. I quit crying when I was nine years old. A brother had hit me. I went to my mother who was reading a book at the kitchen table. Standing next to her, tears sliding down my cheek, she absent-mindedly tapped the ash off her cigarette without looking up from her story. I walked away.

But now, I had no skin to cover my nerve endings.

I devised a plan to squelch my pain. I asked the nurse for a pain pill in the evening. Instead of taking it, I hid it in the nightstand. The next morning, right before the nurse stripped off the dead skin, I asked for another pill. When the nurse turned her back, I took both.

Still, there was no dodging the return of pain. I gave up and cried into the pillow.

When I wasn't hurting, I didn't mind the hospital. I was in a room by myself. I liked the clean white sheets, the smell of disinfectant, and the television all to myself. Mother visited daily. The nurses were kind.

On the third morning of my hospital stay, Dr. Klaas heard me crying. He came into my room and asked me what was wrong.

"It hurts," I said, shocked that he didn't know. I thought others could feel my pain, knew that what they were doing made me hurt and did it anyway.

He told the staff to give me a morphine shot each morning. I lived for that shot.

During my second week in the hospital, more relief came with a long warm bath. I stayed in the white oval womb for hours, warming my insides. I stayed in for as long as I could because when I got out they would pull off more dead skin and wrap my nerves in dressing. The nurses, worried about dehydration, started charting how long I bathed, measuring my fluid input and output. Dr. Klaas chuckled. "You take the longest baths of anybody," he said. "I always know where to find you. We wonder what you do in there for so long."

"Soak," I said, my cheeks flushing. I pulled the hospital sheet up to my neck.

"Here comes my angel," I called out when my friend Matt came through the door to my room. He came with the sunshine in the afternoon that streamed through my window. We played cards, smoked cigarettes, and went for walks throughout the hospital. We laughed when I slammed my hand down in a card game. I had forgotten about the blisters, plump with fluid on my fingers. He didn't stay in my life after my hospitalization. He was there for that moment in time, dissolving into the world as easily as he had sprung from it. When I was older, he'd be a reason why I believed that no matter how bad my life became, the Universe never abandoned me.

On my sixteenth birthday, we had a party in my hospital room. Mother remembered my birthday that year. My grandma and Aunt Annie came from the Twin Cities. Aunt Annie brought me blue moccasins. I touched the leather, saw sky without end.

The next day, two of my older brothers, black-headed Thomas, who hardly spoke, and red-headed David, who talked too much, visited. My joy waned when they asked for beer money. I opened the drawer of my nightstand and gave them dollar bills from the get-well cards I received. Still, I was glad they came. I wondered how much money I owed Mark for tearing off my shirt and saving my life.

After I returned home, my mother's tenderness toward me continued, for a while.

"Listen to this," I told Thomas while we sat in the living room. My mother was out of eyeshot, making dinner in the kitchen.

"Stop hitting me!" I hollered.

Abruptly my mother yelled from the other room, "You leave her alone!"

"See," I said smugly.

I returned to my job of mothering siblings. In addition to birthdays, I also kept track of social security numbers.

I didn't mind being a mother. I enjoyed loving my sisters and brothers and looking after them. My life would have been so different if I had someone looking out for me. On occasion, my brothers did.

I recall my oldest brother, Simon, challenging my mother when I was in third grade. He was in seventh grade, four years older than me.

"Mother, why don't you just let Ann stay home? She doesn't want to go to school."

"No," Mother said. "She has to go to school." She turned back to washing the dishes.

"I want to stay home. I don't feel good," I whined, clutching my stomach. My other brothers had already been driven the four miles to school. Simon had just finished the barn chores.

Mother turned to me. "Ann, you're going to have to ride your bike to school with Simon. I don't have the car, and that's the only way you're going. You can't stay home. Get your bike out of the shed."

Simon put his hand on his hip "Why don't you just let her stay home?"

"No!"

Simon shook his head, muttered under his breath. He reached for my hand. "Come on, Ann."

I pedaled behind him down the long gravel road out of our farmhouse, kicking up dust past the windmill, which later would be torn down, and the barn that would soon burn to the ground. We passed the cow tank, where I would float empty milk pods with my brothers and all of us would jump in when we got hot. Simon and I came to a rise, then coasted to the mailbox, skirting potholes. We took a left, pedaled up the gravel road a quarter mile to the blacktop. At the highway, we turned right and continued on the road, only swerving to the gravel when we heard a car. I did what he did, following his every move.

Now, at sixteen, it was my turn to look after others.

In January, I had to implore our mother to call the school bus company. The driver kept dropping the kids off at the highway, three quarters of a mile from home, when he should have been dropping them off closer to the farm. "Mom, the kids don't have hats and mittens, and they're wearing tennis shoes," I told her. "They're crying and freezing by the time they get home. You have to call. The kids can't cut across the field; the snowdrifts are too high. Mom, you're a social worker. Call!"

I cooked for our family—roast beef, potatoes, chili, cake, meatloaf, and vegetables. Mother came home from work to a plate warming in the oven. She wanted it this way. She grabbed her plate, walked into her bedroom, ate, and read. Or, when it was quiet, she ate alone at the kitchen table, a book in one hand, a fork in the other.

On my hands and knees, I scrubbed the kitchen, hallway, and bathroom floors; a butter knife in one hand, scrubber in the other, and washcloth in the bucket. I moved inch by inch on my knees, calculating that if I started in the corner by my parents' bedroom, I could move down the narrow hallway past my sisters' room, twist into the bathroom, then pass my bedroom and reach the kitchen, where I could change the water, continue, and waddle backwards to the door going outside.

My knees dimpled and blushed. I got satisfaction trading mess for clean, chaos for orderly. The light blue, speckled linoleum shone for a day.

Sometimes I gave up, threw in the towel. I seemed alone in wanting order. But I couldn't stand the mess. The longest I ever lasted was two weeks. A deep thundering began within me, a tossing and turning, and finally I busted out of myself and started throwing things away: clothes, odd shoes, paper, phone books, scattered socks, scrunched cardboard boxes. All of it went into the fiery trash barrel.

When I thought of my mother in her bed reading her books, I felt as if she never cared. But then I remembered her visiting me daily in the hospital. That warmed me inside.

AT THE AIRPORT ARRIVALS, I bounced Antonio in my arms. Large groups of people were going in and out of glass doors. Only a few others, like me, were waiting for travelers. Arrivals, departures, and delays were being announced at short intervals. I imagined Jody lingering to be the last to depart the plane. It would be easier for her. I smelled stale coffee.

Jody stepped down the stairs carrying seven-month-old Crystel in her Baby Bjorn front pack. When we met, she turned Crystel, and we watched the babies eye each other. Were we only imagining that they recognized each other? They had been with each other since Crystel's birth. Antonio smiled, his dark eyes reflecting the light. He reached to stroke his sister's face.

Jody and I hugged, kissed. Our eyes misted over.

Crystel was wearing a pink outfit. Her tongue touched her gum line. Her large, round eyes contemplated Antonio. She was holding Jody's finger; it must have comforted her. Suddenly, Crystel broke into a smile, making her look like an old lady who forgot to put in her dentures.

I hugged Jody tighter. Still embracing, we looked into each other's eyes. I knew that she was thinking the same thing I was. Finally, our family was together.

Jody handed Crystel to me, and I handed Antonio to her. This tiny, tiny baby, only ten pounds at seven months old, had made it to Minnesota. I remembered my promise to take care of her. "Thanks for making it home," I said. I kissed her thin dark hair. Mama Jody gave Antonio a quick kiss, then set him down. I placed our daughter next to him. Antonio scooted to his knees, reached for a railing, and pulled himself up. His wide eyes held Crystel with a look that said, "Me strong. Me Antonio."

Before leaving the airport, we looked for someone to take a photo. I walked out into the passageway, flagged a man down. In the photo, I was holding Antonio and he was looking up at me, worried. Jody was wearing Crystel in her front pack. Crystel was watching Antonio.

Back home, in the living room, my daughter looked up at me from her bouncer, braced up on the end table. She had been changed to a blue footy sleeper with a full-length zipper. Her fine hair fell in wisps around her face. At seven months, her neck muscles and head control should have been strong and steady, not a bobblehead doll. I brought my head close to her so we were nose to nose. She broke into her old-lady smile again. I laughed. Jody snapped a picture. I was meeting my daughter for the first time, really meeting her. She raised her right hand in a "here I am" gesture and I loved her for it.

The next day, our pediatrician measured, prodded, and poked Antonio and Crystel. Antonio received a prescription for a double ear infection. His crying that wouldn't stop was explained. Antonio and Crystel's appointment for a post-adoption medical review was scheduled. There would be hearing and eye appointments and meetings with cranial sacral specialists and an energy worker. Jody and I would use old age, new age, any kind of age, to understand who these children were.

EARLY IN OUR DATING, Jody told me how she noticed I appeared uncomfortable around children. I made an effort not to hold them, not to get close to them.

A therapist I trusted suggested energy work. Together, my energy worker and I tended to the Wounded Child, the Abused Teenager, and the Disowned Adult. During a session, I said to the energy worker, "I want to know why I feel as if I don't deserve children. It might be about Teenager."

I laid on her massage table. I was fully clothed. The energy worker placed her palms, one on top of the other, on my heart, the space between my breasts. At first, her touch was feathery touch. Next, I felt warmth, then strong heat, as if she had just had her hands on the belly of a dog.

"Why don't you phrase a question to Teenager?" she suggested.

"Why do you feel you don't deserve children?" I asked.

"Don't box her in so much. I'm not feeling her. Is she here with us?"

"She's here."

The energy worker adjusted her hands slightly. "Where do you feel her?"

"She's under where your hands are. She's really deep, though. But she's here."

More heat generated under her hands, more heat than either she or my skin was providing. A pulsing activity began, a little slower than my heart pulse. I could feel this pulse. It was a methodical *thump, thump, thump* located at the point of injury—my heart.

"What do you want to say?" I asked Teenager.

Suddenly, I could envision how I once was with infants, toddlers, small children, and my younger brothers and sisters. I had magic. Babies and children were drawn to me. I could calm a crying baby and make children smile and laugh.

"I loved children," I told the energy worker. "They loved me. I always took care of the baby. Ann knew what to do."

"Who is Ann?" the energy worker asked.

"Ann was my birth name. Ann would create games for the kids. I would play with them, be with them. My youngest brother and sisters called me Mom. I'd dress them for school and tend to their hurts." Tears slowly rolled down my cheek. I had legally changed my name and birth certificate, so strong my need to rip my body from my family's womb.

Her window was open. A slight breeze came in.

"Talk to me more about the magic."

I focused on her hands lying above my heart. An image came to me. I was sitting in a circle with children. "I was the Pied Piper," I said. "But after the abortion, after giving up my baby for adoption, I hid my magic deep." I couldn't talk for a minute. "I was afraid"—my voice broke—"If I touched children they would dis . . . dis . . . a . . . appear, or . . . or . . . they would . . . . would die."

A soft rain started to fall.

"Can you feel your magic anywhere in your body?"

"On the right side, deep, under layers and layers. A circle, ah, ah, the size of a half dollar."

"You still have it?"

I paused. "Yes, I still have it."

The energy worker laid her hands on my stomach, moving them in an oval motion around the outline of my belly. Soon I was gasping for air. Heat rose like a volcano. My body trembled. I didn't know if it was the baby or the abortion. I wanted to jump up, run out of her small office.

"Okay, okay," she said soothingly. "It's energy moving, Beth, just let it happen."

"It's the baby," I said. The lava ebbed and flowed inside. I was drawn to the sensation. "Do it again."

"You do it," she said.

I caught my breath. "If you put your hands on top of mine, I think I can do it."

"Okay."

"I never touched myself when I was pregnant."

"Why not?"

"It was a sin. I wasn't supposed to be pregnant. No one talked to me. I couldn't tell anybody that the baby was kicking, that I could feel him moving inside me."

"Are you ready?"

"Where's your hand! Where's your hand!" I kept my eyes tightly closed.

"Right here," she said. "Right here."

Her hand gently landed on top of mine. I brought my palm slowly to my stomach and started to make a circle. I moved an inch, felt a wave, and stopped. I haltingly moved another inch, then another, making it all around.

I lifted my knees and dug my heels into the massage table. I was having the baby all over again.

Even with the rain, birds were chirping outside her window. The faint scent of lilac was in the air. My sister, Patricia, ten years younger than me, was an infant in my arms. I was ten again, cradling her, quieting her cries.

AFTER OUR FOURTH MEDICAL appointment with the babies and after our fourth assurance that Antonio's level of activity was normal, that Crystel's physical, cognitive, and motor development would catch up over time, Jody and I relaxed.

I sat on the couch and held Antonio. I routinely lifted the elbow that was jabbing my breast, maneuvered him to the other side of my body. My chest was dough and Antonio's body the rolling pin. Comfort to him was his body pressing hard against his mothers. We soon learned that his gregarious, demanding, and loud nature silenced Crystel. Even in photographs, Antonio was the one people's eyes were drawn to, and no one could help but smile back at his alluring beam.

Antonio watched Jody holding Crystel in the oversized chair. He crawled off my lap and over to hers. Held his hands up. Whined. Jody set Crystel down, picked up Antonio.

Cold air swept in under the front door.

"I wouldn't do that if I were you," I said. I turned the thermostat up a notch. Sealed the door with a towel.

"Wha—?"

I interrupted her. "Crystel's not going to trust you."

Jody gave me a questioning look.

Crystel was lying on her tummy, her arms outstretched, flying like an airplane.

"What, what should I do?"

"Tell Antonio that he'll have to wait."

Crystel's survival mechanism was to be lifeless, not seen, not heard, and not to show any need. Though she was home, she hadn't yet decided to exist. I studied her fine black hair. I swore that I could see strands of gray. I was old before my time, too. I learned to not count on my parents.

When Jody and I held her, Crystel patted us on our shoulders with a tap, tap, tap as if we were the ones who needed the love. She often placed the back of her palm to her head in a "woe is me" gesture. She started striking her breast as if she was saying, "*mea culpa*, my nature is flawed." When she lay on her tummy, her eyes followed us as we walked away, but she did not cry. She didn't ask to be fed.

We had to make her need us. We had to make her want us.

In my family, we toughened each other up. Taught each other not to cry, not to want, and not to need.

Every night at bedtime, Jody and I touched Crystel's cheek lightly, rubbed her brow and ears, let our fingers play through her hair and told her how lucky we were.

At first, she shrugged us off and turned her head toward the wall. Little by little, her body softened. A night came when she rolled in our direction. An afternoon came when she cried when we walked out of the living room. A day came when she was as loud and demanding as her brother.

WITHIN WEEKS OF THE INFANTS coming home, I ached to hear them say thank you. A grunt. I joyfully would accept a grunt in acknowledgement of our sleepless nights, of our exhaustion, of how much care they took. Was this too much to ask? I sniveled, knowing it was. The children couldn't speak.

Strangers asked, "Do they know Spanish? Do you have to teach them English?"

I wanted to shout, "Do any babies know how to speak?!" But instead, I said politely, "Crying is a universal language."

I couldn't figure out why Antonio and Crystel took so much work. Didn't I parent my younger siblings? Wasn't I the one tending to them, feeding them, being there for them? How was it that two infants could be more work than what I was doing as a teenager?

Jody and I didn't know how to ask each other for help. While one mom tended to both babies, the other stood to the side, waiting for an invite. If I offered to assist, I was worried Jody would be offended, that she'd think that I didn't think she was a good mom. If she wanted help she'd ask, I'd think. But, really, she wanted me to read her mind; I should know what she needed. I thought she should be just like me and ask for what she wanted. I leaned against the wall not offering aid, thinking, *Jody is such a good mother. She tries so hard.*

Finally, two crying babies were too much for one mom. Desperation drove us to communicate. We began to share notes, offer suggestions to each other, and to question the parenting books we were reading.

All the books said that Antonio and Crystel sleeping in the same room would comfort them. At naptime, instead of sleeping, they'd talk and play. At night, Crystel cried long enough to wake Antonio. After he woke, it was her signal to go back to sleep, while he cried for hours. In the meantime, Jody and I were drained.

One day while Jody was at work, I had had it. Enough was enough. The children weren't napping. This meant I would have two over-tired babies in the afternoon. I went into a frenzy, took apart a crib and stacked it in the hallway. I rushed to our bed, pulled off the mattress, dragged it to the top of the basement stairs and pushed it down the steps. The babies watched me wide-eyed. Images of me being awoken at night by a bed being thrown out of my parents' bedroom and Mother screaming, "Goddamn it, George, get out of here, go sleep someplace else!" came to me. I ignored the memory.

From then on, Antonio and Crystel had their own bedroom, directly above ours on the main floor. During the night when my eyes opened, though at first I didn't hear anything, I knew it was for a reason, just as it was when I was growing up. I waited a second, then another, then heard a baby whimpering. If it was Jody's turn to get up, I nudged her. Once upstairs, if one of us wanted help, we'd stomp on the floor three times. If the sign wasn't given, the person in bed could continue to rest. Since we moved the babies to their own bedroom, one baby would sleep through the other's crying.

It was peaceful to have only one infant crying at a time.

Jody and I both worked and were taking turns being the stay-at-home mom.

One afternoon when I arrived home, Jody was holding both babies in her arms. Crystel was wiggling so hard, I was afraid she'd slip out of Jody's embrace. Jody handed her to me. My daughter kissed me (I was sure it was a kiss) with her wide-open mouth, swallowing my nose, splotching my forehead, cheek, and arm.

Crystel learned how to receive love and maybe we should teach her how to kiss with pursed lips, but I didn't want to. I loved what made her *her*. She was my girl.

Antonio greeted me from Jody's other arm with the same toothy smile as he did the first time I met him. He leapt into my free arm, so excited that he was nipping at my shoulders with his teeth. "No bite, Antonio. No bite," I said.

Jody was a quality manager for a software company while I worked as a human resources manager. My company was consolidating our printing plant with a new location and I was laying off 340 employees. Abigail, my coworker, was being laid off from the printing plant and was licensed to be a daycare provider. She and her husband bought a home specifically for her daycare business.

During our visit to the daycare, Abigail demonstrated for Crystel how to press a button, slide a switch, and turn a dial to hatch a pop-up chick, turtle, or toucan. "Now it's your turn," she said. The lights, fun sounds, and music held Crystel's attention. "Do you think we'll hear a squeak when you press the button?" Abigail asked. Abigail explained to us how the toy would encourage Crystel's development of fine motor skills. She directed Antonio to a "Laugh and Learn, Fun with Friends" musical table. Antonio tottered around the four corners of the table. Each had an entire interactive learning center with lights and a friendly character who invited Antonio to play. Antonio could learn letters, numbers, counting, first words, colors, shapes, opposites, and animals in English and Spanish.

At the end of my workday, I rushed to daycare. After collecting the babies, before I had even gone a mile, Antonio was sobbing. Crystel was watching him. Before I could say, "Oh no, not you, too," she burst into tears. I put my blinker on, pulled over onto a side street. First, I lifted Antonio out of his car seat. "Buddy, it's okay. We're going home now. It's okay." I pulled him tight, kissing him on the cheek and head. His sorrow was deep. "Mama always comes back for you," I said. I imagined Antonio holding his breath all day.

His sobs reached into me, pulling at memories. My vision blurred; I gulped for air. My tears fell on his head. Ever since the infants had come home, I hadn't been able to keep my emotions in check. Their pain and sadness cut me. But, then again, it was safe to cry with them. They couldn't talk. They couldn't tell anybody that Mama Beth cried.

I was ten years old. Mother was having another baby. I was staying at Aunt Kate's with my two younger sisters, four and two years old. I pulled them to the shed in a wagon. Once inside, I sat next to them and cried. I missed our mom. Catherine told Aunt Kate, who told Aunt Flora. I was ashamed to miss my mother. I was ashamed that I cried.

My voice broke, "I understand, honey. I understand." I bounced Antonio gently up and down, holding him tight, our hearts beating next to each other. He sobbed and sobbed, and I cried with him.

The neighborhood was peaceful. There was no one honking at me to get going. I heard children playing ball in a field.

Even when Mother wasn't having a baby, I was occasionally sent away to stay with Aunt Kate or Aunt Flora. Mother told me that she wanted to give me a break from my brothers. I felt discarded, a cast-off, one too many and not the right gender. I was gut-wrenchingly homesick and afraid of what was happening back home. There was no one to keep order. No one to take care of my siblings. A barn or house could burn down. Somebody could die.

In third grade, staying at my Aunt Flora and Uncle Albert's house, I got out of bed and walked downstairs, sobbing, my little body shaking.

"I want . . . want . . . to go home."

Aunt Flora and Uncle Albert turned away from the nightly news.

My aunt slowly leaned forward in her recliner. "Let me get you some Seven-Up, honey. It's late."

"I . . . I . . . want to go home."

"I'll call your mother in the morning, after I take you to school."

The next day I was playing Red Rover, Red Rover with the other eight– and nine-year-olds. But I also kept an eye out for my mother's car. St. Francis School didn't have bus service and my mother would be picking up my brothers.

Mother pulled up, jerked the car to park. I ran to the station wagon and jumped in the middle of the backseat. Brothers squeezed in. I was stuck tight in the middle. Right where I wanted to be.

At that moment, Aunt Flora drove up, parking on the other side of the street in front of St. Francis Church.

"Ann, why don't you go with Aunt Flora to Red Wing?" Mother said. "She'll bring you home after shopping."

"No." I wouldn't take my eyes off the floorboard. The only way that I was going home was staying right where I was.

"She'll take Patrick, too."

I crossed my arms. "No."

Patrick, my second-oldest brother, reached over a brother and slugged me on the arm. "Get out, Ann, goddamnit."

Shopping in Red Wing was a rare treat.

I still refused, even after he whacked me on the head.

I didn't care and I didn't cry.

AFTER COMFORTING ANTONIO, I took Crystel out of her car seat and held her until she quieted. "It's okay, sweetie pie. It's okay. It's hard when Antonio is sad, isn't it?" I knew in this moment that daycare was out. One of us would have to quit our job.

"ARE THE CHILDREN TWINS?"

I turned to the woman standing behind me in the grocery line. "No, they're six weeks apart." Immediately after answering, I felt apprehensive. Simply stated, my answer didn't speak of the bond that the babies already had with each other and the bond that I wanted them to have. I corrected myself. "They're brother and sister." I straightened cans and repositioned food in the cart. Antonio and Crystel were in a red double stroller, babbling to each other.

"Oh, they're adopted, then," the woman said. "They're not really brother and sister. They're not from the same family."

I glanced at the rain outside. How was I going to manage getting the babies and groceries to the car? I put the chocolate-covered almonds for Jody on top of the frozen peas. There wasn't any baby food in the cart. The babies wouldn't eat it. Instead, there were bananas, a carton of cottage cheese, salad fixings, muskmelon, and hot dogs.

"They're brother and sister," I said. "We're a family." I moved the warm rotisserie chicken away from the cottage cheese. Antonio and Crystel appeared to be paying no attention to the conversation.

I wanted Antonio and Crystel to have a lifelong bond, different from what I had with my brothers and sisters. *No one can understand you like you guys can understand each other. You're adopted, you're Guatemalan, and you have two moms. Whom else do you know with that history?*

I was now the stay-at-home mom. Jody's company offered domestic partnership benefits and mine didn't. At dinner, I filled her in on our trip to the grocery store. I didn't want to lie and tell people Antonio and Crystel were twins. "But, I also don't like where the truth takes our conversation," I said.

"But you're not lying if you say they're twins," she said. "I read in the *Adoptive Families* magazine that Antonio and Crystel fit in a category called like-twins, pseudo twins, and artificial twins. Children in one family who are less than nine months apart in age."

"Strangers are going to know more about Antonio and Crystel's adoption story than they do. And that's just not right," I added.

"That's a terrible way for them to learn about themselves," she agreed.

I went on, "After the grocery store, I stopped at Walgreens for medicine. Standing in line, someone asked me where they were from."

"What did you say?"

"I said . . . ah . . . Richfield."

Jody laughed.

I stacked dishes. "How long do Antonio and Crystel have to belong to us to be a part of our family, to be from our family? If they are always from Guatemala, will they always be displaced people? Never truly be at home?"

"Why don't you say the children were born in Guatemala and their home is in Richfield?"

I carried the mound to the sink. "Guatemala in Richfield?"

LATER THAT WEEK I WAS at the gas station filling up.

"How much did they cost?" a mother asked. "I've heard they're expensive."

I pulled the receipt out of the slot. I cleared my throat, and then coughed. "I don't remember."

There was a strong smell of gasoline and exhaust.

I had just gotten in a conversation wreck with the children, not knowing yet if they were harmed. I wanted to rush to their sides, tell them how wanted they were. I would have gladly given all of my money to be their mom.

Buckled in their car seats, they were safe. I was the one who couldn't get untangled from the words.

No matter how often I practiced answering questions about Antonio and Crystel, I was never prepared. An unexpected question startled me. To the person talking, I might not appear shocked at all. I grew up learning to show no sign, no hint, and no emotion of what I was feeling, regardless of how mindboggling the wreckage.

———————————

ONE AFTERNOON, MY DRUNK DAD crawled up the steps into our farmhouse. It was unbelievable to me, yet there he was. I was twelve years old. No one reached down to help or to hold the door open for him. I didn't know if we were pretending that we didn't see him or if we were just ignoring him. That evening, I noticed the dark stain of urine on the front of his blue overalls.

A month later, it was late August. Pumpkins were ripening on vines, lying on their side in the garden. The sun, not yet done with summer, warmed the land. It was morning and the sheepshearer pulled into our driveway. Dad and I got into the sheepshearer's truck. I was excited, even though I had to sit on his lap. Dusty puffs of gathered wool, crumpled paper, shortened pencils, and a toolbox sat where I wanted to be— in the middle of the cab. I tried not to smell my dad's mix of Copenhagen, farm, and whiskey.

We were driving to our other farm, the homestead, where the sheep grazed in our fields. I was hoping Aunt Kate, dad's sister, was home. She lived on the homestead by herself. Her house was warmed by a potbelly stove in the kitchen. She'd greet me with a warm and worried smile. There was sure to be a treat offered: an ice-cream bar, hot buttered popcorn, or a root beer fizzy in a glass of well water.

Dad was talking to the sheepshearer. I was staring out the window, uncomfortable in his lap. I had never sat on my dad's lap or even been this close to him. Our family paid him no mind. Suddenly he moved his hands, touched my nipples through my t-shirt. I froze. He rubbed his thumb and fore-finger around my nipples, around and around. My heart raced. The chipped black toolbox was twenty-four inches wide and had a large metal latch. Inside were power tools, hand tools, electric and hand shears, cutters, and combs. It weighed half as much as me. I wouldn't even be able to push it sideways to slide over. Besides, the gearshift was in the way.

Rubbing the fabric of my t-shirt back and forth, Dad fon-dled the bumps my tiny nipples made. All the while talking with the sheepshearer. Soon my nipples were irritated and raw. His fingers were sandpaper.

My face was burning red. I hoped the sheepshearer didn't see, but how could he not? I wasn't daydreaming anymore about cotton candy, corn dogs, Ferris Wheels, or Aunt Kate. I was Nothing sitting on Nothing's lap. What would it be like to have one more person touching me? How would that work, a brother one day, then my dad the next, and then another brother? My twelve-year old mind was like that: I took a problem, whisked it through an endless list of possibilities, and when I locked onto a solution, I tried it. If the answer didn't work or stopped working, I put the problem back in the cylinder and searched again, not stopping until the cylinder fixed on another answer. That's how I figured out how to live through my brothers' rapes—stone-body, impenetrable mind, never speaking.

We pulled into the homestead. Aunt Kate's house was quiet. There were no lights on. I opened her back door, walked past the wood box. Her kitchen door was latched. There was no use knocking. She wasn't home.

I wandered aimlessly. My mind would not click on a solution.

I wouldn't tell my mother about Dad. I didn't want to be the one who tipped her over her edge. She was all we had. Besides, I had already told her about my brother raping me when I was nine and she punished me. I swore that I'd never tell her again, no matter how bad it got.

The cylinder stopped, fixed on an answer: *If my dad keeps touching me, I'll kill myself.*

AFTER A COUPLE DAYS of being closed inside with Antonio and Crystel, I was desperate. I had lost my professional identity. As a human resources manager, I knew who I was and what I was about. At best, most of the time with the children I was guessing.

Lugging the babies to the YMCA would be accomplishing something. The babies weren't yet comfortable being left alone with other caregivers. I knew that our trek would only allow me to place my back against the wall of the nursery and watch them crawl around while they played with the toys. Today, that was enough.

I packed the car with everything we would need while Antonio and Crystel were distracted with their exersaucers. First, I carried Crystel quickly to the car and placed her in her car seat. She whimpered. "It's okay, Crissy, we're only going a short way." I ran back to get Antonio. When he saw Crystel was sad, his eyes got red and puffy. By the time I had him buckled in, both babies were bawling. Still, I climbed in the driver's seat. We could do this.

I had both hands on the steering wheel. The car was running. Loud weeping and convulsive gasping was coming from the back seat. I turned to look at them. Snot was running out their noses, water streaming down their faces. All I wanted to do was go to the Y and watch them play. Twisted in my seat, staring at them, I gripped the steering wheel tightly. "Shut. The. Fuck. Up. Or, I'll send you back to Guatemala." Finally, I threw up my hands. "All right, all right, goddamn it. We aren't going." I yanked open their car doors. "See, we're staying."

After unbuckling Antonio and Crystel, I sat them on the front lawn under the shaded apple tree. All three of us were sniveling now.

They would always be ten months old. They'd never change. I sat on the stoop with my head in my arms. I couldn't do this. I'd have to tell Jody that she was going to have to be the stay-at-home mom. I was going to have to get a job.

If I drank, I sure would like to have a drink at this moment. If I smoked, I sure would like a cigarette. But I hadn't had a drink since I was nineteen and I hadn't smoked since I was twenty-six. All I had was my forty-five-year-old miserable self and these two bawling babies.

The summer day heated up.

All of a sudden, the cylinder clicked on an answer. I took a blanket out of the car and spread it close to Antonio and Crystel. Inside the garage, I took a red plastic sled down from the rafters. After running water into the sled from the outside faucet, I pulled it to the babies. I slid the sled onto the blanket. I batted the water with my hands. Antonio's and Crystel's eyes grew wide. I splashed again. Water sprayed onto Crystel. She laughed and shined her old-lady smile. She clasped her hands and swayed back and forth. Antonio slapped the water hard with his fists. His eyes sparkled. With his toothy grin, he crawled into the sled, spilling water over the sides.

I stared at the two of them. Maybe, just maybe, I could do this.

PART
TWO

PART

TWO

A T THE SOCIAL SECURITY OFFICE, I LOOKED OVER THE
waiting room. A half-dozen people sat far apart from
each other. A woman shook off her raincoat before
draping it over the back of a chair. An older man removed his
Twins ballcap and slapped it on his leg. I hadn't brought an
umbrella, either. I took my windjacket off, gave it a shake. It
was only misting when I left the house, and besides, I didn't
believe in umbrellas. Umbrellas and sandals were for city folk.

I wiped my feet on the entrance mat. Ever since the babies
had come home, I had insisted on being the mother who filled
out forms, whether we were at the pediatrician's, a clinic, or a
government office. I was taking back my identity. I refused to
be invisible any longer. With great delight, I put my name
where it said "Mother."

There was a wait. I was prepared. The *Best of Prairie
Schooner* was in my backpack. I had been reading Richard
Russo's short story, "The Dowry."

A stoic female guard motioned me to take a number and
turn off my cell phone. I pulled the arrow and glanced down
at the pink paper, number seventy. After flipping my backpack
on a chair, I dug for the forms. Applying for Antonio and
Crystel's social security cards should be easy.

There were three parts to question one: Name to be shown on social security card, full name at birth if other than above, and other names used.

Darn. I reached for my phone, tucked deep inside my jacket, and approached the guard.

"How do you know what number they're on?" I asked.

Without changing expression or even lifting her head, the large black woman pointed to the wall. Number sixty-five was highlighted in red. "You can't use your phone here. You need to step outside."

Before walking into the hall, out of curiosity, I checked if she was armed. She was not.

Jody answered on the first ring. She didn't berate me when I asked, "What were Antonio and Crystel's middle and last names at birth?" I loved her for that. Jody knew what she had gotten into partnering with me and what I brought to our union. If this were her task to complete, she wouldn't have had to call me. She had taken file cabinets to appointments like this.

"I'll have to go upstairs, just a second."

When Jody returned, she told me that Crystel's middle name was Rocio. She had two last names, Soto and Argueta. Antonio didn't have a middle name. He had two last names, too—Amperes and Sesam. "Wait," she said. "Amperes ends in a 'Z.' No, maybe it's an 'S.'"

I interrupted her. "Thanks, I'm good."

Jody would anguish over a "Z" or an "S." That's what made her such a good employee and mother. Me, I didn't like to follow rules. This was just government paperwork. There were government laws that said Jody and I shouldn't be married. It was not yet November 2003, when Massachusetts became the first United States jurisdiction to license and recognize same-sex marriages.

Returning to the waiting area, I glanced at the dingy off-white wall—still number sixty-five. I sat, placed my back against the bones of the chair, and studied the social security application. My relaxed jaw slowly clenched, my spine straightened, and I scratched and scribbled, tossed the forms aside, picked up my book, and turned to "The Dowry."

I lingered, my finger marking the page. If Jody and I died without a will, our assets—what we brought into our union and our financial gains while in our relationship—would be divided amongst our immediate family. Our immediate family didn't include each other, though we had been a couple for over six years. My face heated up.

WE MET THE SUMMER of 1997. A friend knew a woman who wanted to run a marathon. "Would you give her some pointers?" she asked me. I arranged to meet Jody at Lake Harriet in Minneapolis.

"You'll complete the Twin Cities marathon and not be injured if you train with me," I told Jody. "I'm a slow runner, but I finish."

Jody was the youngest of six kids. Her father worked as a loan officer for his father's finance business until it was sold. She was a tomboy as a kid, running barefoot through the woods behind their house. She had been married for ten years. She and her husband didn't have children. They remained friendly after the divorce.

In our mid-thirties, mile after mile, we walked, jogged, and ran into a committed relationship.

Nineteen miles of trails and a thousand acres of woodland, grassland, and wetland habitat at Hyland Lake Preserve in Bloomington were our playground. Conversation came easily, jogging the woodchip trails surrounding the lake, dashing up a narrow rocky path to the top of a hill, and weaving through long prairie grasses. During runs, we talked about our families, our pasts, what we wanted in our future. Coming around a bend, I pointed to an owl gliding toward a tree. We stood side by side, looking upward into the branches. We watched as the owl turned her head toward a rustling in the grass. Our similarities in backgrounds were striking. Both of us stopped using alcohol and drugs, participated in twelve-step programs, began individual and group therapy while in our teens. As adults, we remained in recovery programs. Our beliefs, values, and morals were similar. They strengthened our relationship as the running strengthened our legs and lungs.

I dated men until I was thirty. I could understand Jody loving and marrying a man. I loved men, too. But years of abuse by my brothers made intimacy with a man difficult.

"I'll race you to the top of the hill," I said.

Jody won easily. I wasn't used to a woman being stronger or faster than I was.

After long runs, we returned to my house. Afternoons were spent reclining in the daybed, warmed by the sun. We laid in companionable silence or chattered like the birds that we heard through the screen window. There wasn't anything in that room from other houses that I had lived in. No baggage.

"Does my past bother you?" I asked.

She contemplated the question. For once, I waited in the silence. The birds were even quiet.

Jody shook her head. "I was attracted to you because you believe in the world despite all you've been through." She paused. "You have a determination to take care of yourself beyond all else."

A squirrel was under the bird feeder, eating scattered seeds.

"You have such an interest in self-discovery," she added.

"NUMBER SEVENTY."

I wedged the book in my backpack, hitched the load to my shoulder. With the forms twisted in one hand, I stepped heavily toward the voice that sang from behind a divider. A woman motioned me to sit. She was in her thirties and of East Indian descent, or was it Somalian or Ethiopian? Or, who was I kidding? I really didn't have a clue. The fact that she wasn't white and that she wasn't African-American disappointed me. I assumed the person I was talking to was an immigrant. My shoulders drooped, bringing my backpack to a plop on the floor. How would she react to me saying my children had two moms? I was aware that I was categorizing her, putting her into a box.

"What can I do for you today?"

I was surprised at her perfect English. Maybe this would be okay. "I'm here to apply for social security cards for my two adopted children, Antonio and Crystel." I passed her their birth certificates, their Guatemalan passports, their permanent resident cards, and the social security applications. "They have two moms." I pointed to "mother" on the application. "That's me. I crossed out where it said 'father,' wrote 'other mother,' and added my partner. Then I crossed out 'father's social security number' and put her social security number."

I hoped she would detect the ridiculousness of all this, the energy I had already had to expend and the anger I had swallowed. She wore a crystal butterfly necklace. I studied the small bursts of purple, blue, pink, and clear crystal that dangled from the gold-plated chain. Jody and I tried to have a baby on our own. I twice failed at insemination. During the time Jody was inseminating, I gave her a Tibetan quartz crystal. The crystal was a family of crystals, four and a half inches long and one and a half inches wide. Jody meditated with this crystal and laid it on her belly. She carried it in her pocket and held it during her sleep. Jody failed to conceive five times. When we learned that our little girl's name was Crystel, we related it back to the precious stone.

"Um, just a moment," the woman said. She stood and then stepped to the left, behind a divider.

I could hear her voice, but I couldn't make out what she was saying. She had interrupted her co-worker, who was helping a short, stocky fellow seated next to me. We weren't walled off from each other. I wanted to whisper, "Sorry," or, at the very least if he looked my way, shrug my shoulders. I pushed my backpack farther under my chair. I hoped the ruckus would make him look at me. I wanted an acknowledgement that it was me that they were talking about, that it was my family being discussed. I stared at his profile and sent him daggers: *I'm right here, dude. Turn your head. Look at me.*

The woman returned, then plucked at her keyboard. I was curious if the computer allowed her to change where it said "father's name" to "other mother" but I didn't feel as if I had a right to ask. Her earrings matched her necklace. Over her *tap, tap* on the keyboard, I heard the humming of fluorescent lights. The buzzing began crowding me. I kept telling myself that this was one day, one moment in my life, just one day. Antonio and Crystel would have many days like this, explaining who they were and where they came from and why they had two moms.

I waited for her to detect that I didn't check a box where it stated race/ethnic description. I was supposed to check only one, but this was also voluntary. There was no box for "other." If there were, I would have checked "other" and written in "Guatemalan." To me, even checking the "Hispanic" box marginalized the children. It didn't honor their true indigenous Mayan ethnicity. I knew Jody would just mark "Hispanic" without giving it another thought. I was glad that it was me filling out the forms.

The tapping stopped. "Where did Martin come from?" She indicated the square that read "other names used."

Why do I have to explain? was what I wanted to say, but we needed Antonio and Crystel's social security numbers to file for the $10,160 federal adoption tax credit. "Jody adopted the children first," I explained. "Her married name was Martin. Antonio and Crystel came into the United States under the name of Martin. Jody has since changed her name to di Grazia." Taking a deep, controlled breath, I continued, "At the second-parent adoption, Antonio and Crystel, though named Martin, changed their name to di Grazia. All of us are di Grazias." I walked her through it one more time. "Jody's maiden name was Grady. Her married name was Martin. And now she's a di Grazia."

"Oh, um, just a moment." She stepped behind the wall and again interrupted her co-worker.

If this woman asked where di Grazia came from, should I tell her the name chose to be with us, that it evolved out of a meditation on the Tibetan quartz crystal? That would not go over well, I supposed. My neighbor was a "regular guy in America." He adjusted his glasses, then stretched out his legs. *Hey, guy? Even a cursory glance would do. Just a tiny acknowledgement that we are in the same boat, that it is us against the bureaucracy, us against the system. How about a thumbs up, guy?*

Returning, the tall, slender woman sat down again, and asked, "What was your maiden name?" She placed her chin on her folded hands, waiting for an answer.

"I don't have a maiden name." I gritted my teeth. "My birth name was Ann Elizabeth Smith; I changed it to Elizabeth Ann di Grazia. We are all di Grazias—me, Jody, Antonio, and Crystel."

Another "Oh, um, just a moment" from her. She stared at her computer screen.

I straightened my chair and faced her. I knew our story was complicated, but it wasn't uncommon. Jody was married for ten years to a man before partnering with me. Her maiden name was Grady; her married name was Martin. To not complicate matters, she kept her married name for the adoption. Since I wasn't named on the adoption paperwork, I didn't need to wait. Before the adoptions were final, I changed my birth certificate, social security card, passport, and driver's license to reflect our new family name, di Grazia. Antonio and Crystel became legally mine when we completed a second-parent adoption in Hennepin County.

She continued to stare at her screen. She twirled her hair around her finger.

I remembered that day in Hennepin County, how I let my breath out slowly when Jody stated under oath, in front of a judge, that I had a legal right to Antonio and Crystel. I didn't have any reason to doubt Jody, but we recently had heard of a couple where the legal adopting mother didn't follow through on her promise to allow the other mother to adopt the child.

Finally, she looked up from her monitor. "We won't be able to complete your application today. I need the adoption decree with both parents listed."

"The birth certificates have us listed as parents," I argued. I pointed her to the area where "Elizabeth Ann di Grazia" and "JoAnn Kay di Grazia" were named.

"It doesn't matter. I need the form that you received before you received the birth certificate. Also, we have to mark that they are legal aliens allowed to work and not U.S. citizens until you get a United States passport for them."

Aliens? Aliens are funny green men from a different planet. Allowed to work? They weren't even walking yet. "I couldn't have received the birth certificates without the adoption decree, and I know Crystel came to the United States as a citizen because she came on a different visa."

"It doesn't matter. You need to have a United States passport to show citizenship. Most people wait to get the social security numbers until after they get the passports." She turned her head toward the wall and said, "Number seventy-one."

I was not most people. I reached for my backpack.

Rain was falling steadily. I darted to the car. Sliding into my seat, I slammed the door shut. I was drenched. I put the key into the ignition. A black umbrella poked out from under the passenger seat, which Jody had carefully tucked away.

It occurred to me that she would have been successful in getting the social security cards.

THE RAIN STOPPED. Sunny days tumbled along, one right after another.

At first, I reasoned that I had a simple case of too much sun. There was a little burning in the corner of my eyes. Redness and scaling was on my neck. The rash crept to my cheekbone.

I frowned. "Jody, look at this." I ran a finger down my neck then pointed to my cheek. "What do you suppose this is?"

She winced, drew back from me. "You better see a doctor."

"Well, let's wait. It's not that bad."

The shiny red skin appeared on my inner thigh. It had been a week now and I'd been studying the outbreak's trajectory. I had the cycle down, inflammation, then burning and spreading, layers of skin eaten, then brown skin that I could peel off in strips. *Could I have caught something from the kids?* I asked myself while putting Lotrimin on a reddish area near Antonio's butt. Maybe I had diaper rash? When I closed my eyes, I saw my face, arms, and legs all eaten up.

I called Jody at work. She didn't answer. I left a voicemail. "I have a doctor's appointment"—my voice cracked—"Would you stay with the kids while I go?"

She left me a voicemail saying that she had a meeting, and couldn't I ask someone else?

I called her back. Another voicemail. "I want you to tell work that you have a family emergency and if you can't do that, just let me know . . ." I took a breath. "I want to know how important me . . . and the kids are. And if I'm not important, how bad will the kids have to be hurt for you to leave work? How many stitches?"

I placed the phone in the receiver. I opened the dishwasher and reached for dirty plates and cups from the sink. I fumbled placing the dishware in the slots. Being the stay-at-home mom, I knew the caregiving of the children was up to me. I squeezed a plastic cup in tight between the uprights.

When Jody wasn't at work, she was still at work, her back up against the heat register in the living room and her computer on her lap. I knew that Jody's part was to financially support us, but did she always have to be at work? Blindly, I grabbed silverware from the sink and stuffed them hard into the basket. If she could, she would work twenty-four hours a day. She said her job demanded it. I had been with her long enough to know that her job proved her worth. I maneuvered the tableware awkwardly until they fell into their place. If it wasn't work, it was her biological family she was trying to please.

Antonio and Crystel were napping. Reaching for the frying pan, I reminded myself to not bang the pan and wake the children. I should have soaked it more. The scouring pad I was using scraped at the nonstick Teflon coating on the bottom.

When I was growing up, my mother was embarrassed to be in a situation that she couldn't get out of—no money, a shitload of kids, and a drunk for a husband. What would her mother and siblings say if they ever found out? Were Jody's work and her biological family more important than I was? I scrubbed harder. My mother was caught in fire. The barn burned, the house burned, her daughter burned, what the hell would burn next? I rinsed the pan, winced at the gouges. I wasn't in a situation that I couldn't get out of and neither were the children. Antonio and Crystel would not have the life that I did. I stopped my movements. Was that Antonio? "Here I come, bud." I positioned the frying pan in the drying rack.

Lifting Antonio out of his crib, I shushed him so he didn't wake Crystel. "Let's change your diaper, honey." I laid him on the changing table, reached for a rubber giraffe from the dresser, and handed it to him. Immediately, he put it into his mouth. I reached for a diaper from the Pamper Cruisers Giant Pack before lifting the tape from his soiled diaper. I had developed a method for changing him. Baby boys were known to pee when air hit their genitals. When I was a teenager, I saw a lot of penises. I came to learn the signs that sexual abuse was imminent. First the niceness, the being pleasant, the "I'm your friend." The words moved to "Please, Ann, please?" My body grew cold. My saying "No" did nothing to stop the never-ending "Please, Ann, please?" I was frozen by the time the bartering started. "No, I'll get pregnant. I'll give you a blow job instead."

Antonio took the giraffe's leg out of his mouth, squeezed the body, listening for the bleat he knew would come. He had been teething. The front of his shirt was saturated with drool. He turned the giraffe and put the giraffe's ear in his mouth. After finishing with his diaper, I held him down with one hand while I grabbed a shirt off the top of his dresser with the other.

Crystel was babbling in her crib. I had best hurry, wash my hands, and get Antonio settled in the living room. The burning on my thigh was creeping further up. I willed myself to not touch the area.

THOMAS, MY BROTHER who didn't talk, the one who was in the same high school grade as me, was driving us home one afternoon after school. Suddenly, he turned off the highway and took the back roads, past farm fields and side roads, then pulled close to the ditch. Cornstalks were brown, hard, and brittle in the field. Ears would start dropping on the ground soon and be useless as feed. My stomach cramped. I zipped my jacket up to my neck.

Giving him a blowjob, I was housed between his crotch and the steering wheel, hoping no cars drove by. I didn't mess around because the quicker I was, the sooner this was done. Then I detected movement in his pubic hair. I didn't move my eyes from the spot, studying it. Something was crawling up a hair follicle. I shortened thrusts to keep away from his crotch.

"Thomas, man, err . . . you have, err . . . crabs. Who'd you get them from? I . . . I know you didn't get them from me."

He smiled but didn't speak. My left hand still had the lead in it from the pencil he stabbed me with in third grade. I wouldn't move over and let him butt in front of me to use the pencil sharpener. He didn't say anything then, either. He just stabbed me.

I didn't tell anyone. Not the teacher, not my mother.

I PLACED ANTONIO in his activity saucer. He banged on the musical piano when he was not mouthing the pull handle that activated sounds.

The itchiness of my thigh took me back to Thomas.

"YOU . . . YOU . . . HAVE TO take something for 'em," I said. For Christ's sake, did he think they were just going to magically disappear? "I know someone who has some, err . . . stuff. How can you stand it? You must be itching all the time."

I told my other brothers that I had crabs, that their bed-clothes needed washing. Dragging sheets and blankets from all the beds, I dumped the mass in a huge pile next to the washer. They laughed and poked fun at me, but I remained expressionless and turned the wash dial to "hot." In between putting the roast on at 350 degrees, peeling potatoes, and chopping carrots, I was able to get everything taken care of before Mother came home from work.

CRYSTEL WAS CHANGED and in an exersaucer next to Antonio when Jody pulled into the drive.

"You can count on me to be here for you," she said.

I grabbed the keys, brushed her aside, and walked out the door.

A FEW WEEKS LATER, my sister Margaret called just as Antonio and Crystel went down for a nap.

"Patricia's birthday is on Saturday. Everyone is in town. Let's have a party at your house." Margaret was the tenth child. She was loud, brassy, and blonde. I was nine years old when I started mothering her.

"Margaret?" I paused, looked out the kitchen window at the green grass, the row of pine trees marking our property line. "Could you call back in a few minutes?" What I didn't tell her was that I had to really think about this.

I stepped outside. Looked up at the blue sky. Not a cloud in sight. Next to me was a bed of yellow daylilies. I squatted to pull weeds. Soil dug under my fingernails. I took a deep breath, smelled the churned-up earth.

GROWING UP, MY FAMILY was my life. I belonged. Despite the abuse, my brothers were my best friends and playmates. Born in the middle of seven boys, I wished I were one, too. There wasn't anything they could do that I couldn't. During spring on the farm, water merged from fields, creating a stream behind our barn that made a meandering trip to the creek. Leaping from one ice mound to another, I checked my weight on the overhang that curtained the rushing water. My brothers and I swam in the chilly water under the highway bridge bordering our land. Spring plowing brought rides on the stone boat and seed planter, and fertilizer-sack fires at the end of the field. The soil worked its way into my pores, finding a home. The sun warmed my face and feet as I ran barefoot. When the corn was over my head, we shocked it—one brother driving the tractor, which pulled the machinery that cut, bundled, and tied the stalks. The green bundle was then tossed by another brother onto the wagon for us to stack. Later, we'd drive to the cow pasture, laugh at the cows chasing us, break the bundle, and toss it off the wagon.

During summers, we divided into teams and played the corn game—hiding amongst five-foot-high rows, dodging each other, freeing the prisoners. The best of us hid well, liberating siblings without being discovered. Each year the cornfield was rotated, but the game stayed the same.

Haying season meant the elevator would be stationed at the barn, its green tongue in the mouth of the high window, spitting bales and hay forts. The elevator measured my growth from year to year. It was our swingset, our jungle gym, and our playground. We played tag on its green supports, swung from its bars, did chin-ups. I was the right height when I could finally jump from the lower bar to the very highest and pull myself out of the way from being tagged.

The haymow was our summer and winter playground. Who dared jump or swing off the conveyor belt to the stack of hay below? Who could make the neatest fort, the longest tunnel?

When winter came and night arrived by five o'clock, the barn game was played. It was similar to the corn game, except rows of corn were now rows of cows, twenty-five on each side. Lights were shut off, changing the barn to midnight and shadows. Cows stood or lay in their stanchions, chewing their cuds. It was up to each player how they hid themselves: some lay next to cows, some positioned themselves under a cow that was upright, some squeezed tight into a dark corner.

I was never bored. There were no rules, no place we couldn't play, and no boundaries. We climbed silos, polebarns, and granaries. Summer and winter we slid down roofs, made forts, followed the creek. Every time I climbed a tree and felt its bark rub against my hand, every time I sat on a log and breathed the sun through my skin, every time I smelled the ripe hay or cupped silage in my hand or let oats sift through my fingers, the universe gathered in my cells.

As a child, I had the farm. Always, I had the farm. One hundred and twenty acres of crops, cows, chickens, pigs, ponies, and one donkey. Calves were born, chickens beheaded, innards spilled from a butchered cow, and puppies lapped at a tin of fresh, warm milk. I loved it all.

———————————————

I BUNCHED THE WEEDS TOGETHER; dirt still clung to their roots. Before tossing the cluster into the compost, I took a deep breath and smelled that beautiful earth smell again. In the kitchen, I glanced at the phone, hoping Margaret didn't call me back. I needed more time to think.

ONE SUNDAY MORNING, I stayed home alone with my brother Patrick. Margaret was a newborn. I was nine.

"Come on, kids, we're leaving for church in ten minutes!" Mother yelled. "Michael, get over here. Let me see you. George, get the car started. Goddamn it, George! Aren't you ready yet? You're worse than the kids are. Get out of those barn clothes and get washed up."

Michael walked over to my mother, tucking in his shirt. She straightened his collar, brushed the side of his pants with her hand. "Go sit in the car. You're going in the first car. Do you have all your First Communion stuff? Where's your prayer book? Make sure that white shirt stays clean." Turning from Michael, Mother hollered, "Come on, and let's go! Patrick, get dressed!"

"I don't have any clean pants."

"Wear Simon's."

"I'm not wearing his." He threw up his hands. "They don't fit me."

"Check if there's a pair on—"

"There's not." Patrick stomped his foot.

"Stay home, then, and pick up the living room!" She went into the bathroom. "Ann, come here." Leaning toward the mirror, she held a tube of red lipstick and put some on rapidly, then smacked her lips. "Remember to turn the potatoes on at ten thirty. The roast should be fine." She closed the tube, pulled the drawer out, and dropped it in. "If the baby is hungry, fix her a bottle."

The house was different with no one home. I walked through the quiet rooms. Trying not to make noise, I tiptoed. Patrick was walking up the basement stairs. He was twelve.

"Ann, help me pick up the Sunday paper."

Leaning over, I pulled sheets of scattered newspaper toward me, bunched some in a ball, threw it at him, and dashed away. Patrick sprinted after me through the living room, through the office, through the kitchen, and back to the living room. Round and round we ran. Patrick stopped running. He was taking the cushions from the couches in the office, cramming them in the doorway between the office and kitchen. The barricade wasn't that strong. If I hit them hard enough, the cushions would topple over.

Suddenly Patrick barreled toward me.

Boom! I hit the cushions. They folded but didn't crumple. I scrambled, lifting my skinny legs over. Patrick wrestled me to the floor, cushions scattering. He held me down with his body. He took his fingers and jammed them up my shorts into my twat—because that was what my brothers called it, that was the only name I had for the place he put his fingers.

"Patrick, leave me alone!"

He continued thrusting his finger upward. I throttled from side to side, trying to get him off. "Leave . . . leave . . . me alone . . . I'm telling Mom!" His fingering continued for what seemed like another minute. Then he got up and walked away.

Margaret squirmed in her crib. I checked her diaper and warmed her bottle. I climbed into the crib. My body shook while I held and fed her. Soon it would be all of my brothers, all of the time.

THE PHONE RANG AGAIN. My heart jumped. I turned the faucet off.

"Come on, Ann. It'll be fun!" Margaret said. "We want to meet your babies."

I listened to Margaret talk. Before I reported the sexual abuse in our family to the police, there was a one-for-all-and-all-for-one feeling among us siblings. It was us against you. As damaging as the sexual abuse was, there was a sense of belonging.

"Ann? You there?"

It was just last week that Antonio turned one. Already, he was teeter-totter walking, using dancing hands above his head for balance. Crystel turtled behind her brother, following him around the house and yard mimicking "uck, uck, uck." A few days ago, we had taken the children for a walk when Antonio pointed wildly to the sky, and Jody explained that the big noisy birds were ducks. "Uck," became their favorite word, and they used it for anything that flew. So innocent. But it didn't stop there. "Uck, uck, uck" came over the baby monitor when they woke in the morning. I would never allow their innocence to be threatened . . .

"Ann?"

"Okay," I finally said. Dirt from washing my hands made a trail to the drain.

I picked up the scattered toys in the living room. I retrieved the mail out of the mailbox. I had written a letter to Margaret six months ago, when I learned Patrick was staying at her house and babysitting her three young children. In the letter, I described my childhood, teenage, and adult experiences with Patrick. I also included two children's books about touch.

After she received the package, she called me. "Ann, I burnt the books you sent me."

"Margaret, they're children's books—"

"How could you?" she demanded.

"Margaret," I insisted. "Your two– and four-year-olds need to learn about touch."

"I burnt them, Ann. And don't ever mention this to my husband or children." She took a quick drag of her cigarette. "I ripped up your letter without even reading it. My brothers are my friends. Patrick is their favorite uncle."

Did Margaret place the two small picture books on the cement in the middle of her garage and then stuff Sunday funny papers underneath, around, on top, and then dump gas on the entire mess? Gas is what we used on the farm to start all our brush fires. Following one long last drag of her cigarette, did she flick the fiery butt smack in the middle? *Swoosh.* It was gone. Just like the barn and the house.

I paused at the doorstep, mail in hand, and looked once more at the daylilies. Rugged, adaptable, beautiful, they endured in a garden for many years with little or no care.

Maybe now that my parents were dead things could be different with my brothers and sisters. Maybe we could be buddies. Maybe Antonio and Crystel could be the magnet that brought us together. Maybe it was only our parents that were crazy and without them, get-togethers could be safe.

I knew Jody would support me in having my brothers and sisters at our house. She'd even make the refreshments.

———————————

ON THE DAY OF THE PARTY, my younger brothers and sisters and their families swarmed the three-season porch, dropping sport bags, shedding clothes, and yanking swim diapers over their children's chubby, short legs. The mob made a beeline past the baked beans, past the vegetable tray, the fruit bowl, the sandwiches, and birthday cake to the backyard swimming pool.

I stood in the breezeway waving to my brother, Michael, my childhood best friend. Across the lawn he rushed, a bull in charge of his pasture, though it was my home. His stubby physique hoofed toward me. I held my ground and met his lunge with a quick, hard hug.

"How are you? How was the drive from Oregon?"

"Hellish. Van broke down over the Dakotas. We had to take an extra day. I bet you heard us a few blocks away. Damn muffler fell off and I had to find a junkyard. Shit. I thought I had tied it up good enough."

I scanned the parked vehicles. "Why do you have cardboard taped on your windows?"

"For my three boys to watch the VCR and sleep." Michael's wife skittered past the porch, not saying a word. "Hey, I'm leaking oil, but it's all right. I'm on the street." Michael palmed a turkey sandwich. "Hey, let me see your kids."

I turned to the porch window. I had a view of Jody placing bits of watermelon on Antonio's and Crystel's highchairs.

Michael slapped me on the back and rubbed his jaw with his other hand. "Big sister? Tell me how motherhood is. You don't believe in all that loving kindness bullshit, do you? Hell, I belt my ten-year-old every six months or so. They need it. Have to have it. Toe the line." He patted his stomach. "I have to get after my wife sometimes. She's harder on the kids than I am. I have to stop her. She loses control."

I doubled over slightly, desperate for a sign that Michael was kidding. "Don't you remember when Mom slashed your hand with a knife?" I turned to center the sandwich platter on the long narrow table, nauseated with the memory. I stacked the toppled sandwiches.

"You just wait. You'll find out soon enough. Hey, it's time for the pool!" he shouted.

The weather was perfect for swimming. It was sunny, eighty-six degrees, no breeze. But I shivered.

I walked over to the crabapple tree, where Jody and the children were. Our eyes met. I hugged her and kissed each child's head. I mulled over my conversation with Patricia the day before. I cried when she told me that our Baptist sister, Catherine, disciplined her three children by having them go to their bedroom, pull down their pants, and wait while she got the belt. "It's the will of God," she explained.

"Hey, get off that diving board! I'm first!" Michael yelled to his ten-year-old son. "Don't you know that I'm the champion? Just ask your aunt. Isn't that right, Ann? No one else can do a gainer."

In full gainer, the diver leaves the board facing forward and completes a full backward somersault to enter the water feet first with his back to the diving board.

The hot afternoon sun bounced off the water.

"Show us, big shot," our brother Paul said while pulling off his shirt. He stretched his arm behind his back. Paul, a year younger than Michael, was the quiet, loyal one. Often, the three of us would throw corn or eggs at cars from our hideout near the Highway 63 bridge. Or put a purse filled with cow shit in the middle of the road and watch cars and farm trucks come to a screeching stop. One afternoon, my heart pumped wildly when Paul yelled from our lookout, "Hey! A fire truck is parked on the bridge!" The firefighters were putting out a smoky grass fire we had started underneath.

Michael stepped up on the diving board, staggered, balanced himself, and marched to the end of the board. He squinted, looked into the water, then stepped back two paces.

The murmuring of voices fizzled around the pool and the smell of popcorn settled in the air. Pine tree branches, usually noisy with sparrows, weren't rustling. Standing on the white of the diving board, Michael scratched his red hair. His legs shook. After rubbing his potbelly, he took a few quick steps, bounced, and completed a full somersault backwards.

Michael's son stepped onto the diving board. He ran and dived into the water.

"Jesus, did you see him do that?" Michael said, climbing up the ladder. "I didn't even know my kid could swim. Hey, great dive, kid!"

Michael was oblivious to the fact that we were all staring at him. He was right—none of us could do a gainer.

"Beth, I'm going in the house for a moment," Jody said. "Would you keep an eye on Antonio and Crystel?"

"Sure." Antonio rocked on his tippy toes to the gardening hose, touching the dripping water. Crystel splashed in the hard plastic kiddy pool. Patricia stepped forward to greet me. I uncrossed my arms and received her hug.

"Thanks for having us all, Beth. It's a great day. And the kids love it." Patricia was the only sibling who called me Beth. The others wouldn't recognize that I legally changed my name.

The peaceful moment was broken when Michael's wife screamed at her kids. "I'll kick your ass if you don't get out of the pool right now!" Her three boys, stair-step blonds, were hanging on the rope that divided the little end from the big end of the pool.

Quickly, I glanced at Antonio and Crystel. Antonio dropped the garden hose and turned toward the noise.

"Patricia, would you watch Crystel?" I grabbed Antonio before he reached the pool steps. "Come on, bud. I have you. Do you want to swim? Let's go in." Antonio propelled his arms, kicked his feet in the air. I set him in the water, holding his torso.

"Here Ann, let me have him," Michael said.

My eyes widened. A short while ago, Michael fed my sister's baby, spooning too quickly, scraping his chin, and forcing the squash back into his mouth. Antonio's dark eyes were big and round. His small compact body tightened and he pushed himself against my waist when Michael reached for him.

"No," I said.

"Come on. Let me have him." Michael grabbed for Antonio. I backed away, lifting him into my chest.

"No."

"Come on."

"No." I took another step back. "He's my son."

"Look. You've made him suspicious of me."

"Well, maybe he should be."

"Fuck you, then." Michael backhanded water at me, turned and swam to the deep end. His splash hit my side as I spun away.

The reunion finally ended with doors slamming and "get in the car!" clawing at the air.

I walked into the dining room. My eyes were drawn toward a corner. What was that on the floor? Inching slowly toward the hutch, past the Queen Victoria chair, my head jutted forward, drawing my body. Was it something the cats brought in? I studied the uneven piles. Were they the entrails of a bunny, a chipmunk, or parts of a bird? Kneeling, my chest, face, and upper torso tightened. My neck muscles bulged and pulsated. With my nose scrunched, I willed myself to study the mess. A putrid smell rose up.

It was shit. Three uneven lumps of shit.

I went to the bathroom for toilet paper. I shook my head in disgust. *Let there be no mistake,* the shit said. *You need to stop expecting your brothers and sisters to be any different from what they are. You can't control what comes into your house, into your family, when you invite them in.*

I shook my head, staring at the shit. *Let there be no mistake. You will be the one left to clean up.*

I picked up the shit. Threw it away.

———————————————————

JUST BEFORE HER AFTERNOON NAP, two-year old Crystel was having a fit—stuck, superglued to the floor. Wilted, fragrant lilacs bunched at her feet.

I wanted to pull her into my arms, cradle her in the rocking chair, all the while crooning that I loved her. I didn't pick her up. If I had, then this would have encouraged the next level of her fit—flailing body parts accompanied by ear-piercing squalls. Her body would stiffen. Her head would loll back. It was as if she was possessed by some inner demon, one that only she could work out of her system. I had learned to ask first. Until she answered in the affirmative, I left her glued wherever she was.

"Crystel, I'd like to hold you. You look as if you are having a hard time. Can I hold you?" I picked up the purple lilacs. "Smell the pretty flowers? We could pick more."

My offer did not stop her. Now I was at that point where I had to interject a stern warning, "Don't. Have. A. Fit." I did this as much out of fear as hating to be in the same room with her when she was exorcising her torment. I learned that as long as I kept talking to her and didn't touch her, I could usually head off these moments.

"You don't have to do that, Crystel. I'm right here. I want to help you."

When I said this, I realized they were the same words I had heard my energy worker say to me.

————————————

I WAS LYING ON the massage table on my back with my eyes closed, the energy worker standing at my feet. She quickly rubbed her hands together. The scent of lilac bushes in full bloom floated in through her open window. She moved with certainty to the top of my feet, lightly touching them. I soaked in the warmth of her hands.

Her hands lifted slightly above my feet. My attention drew to the rumbling in my lower abdomen and the fire in my throat.

"What do you see?" I asked.

"What do you see?" was her response.

I smiled. I learned to trust my senses by noting that we recognized the same energy. With my eyes still closed, I answered, "I feel a disturbance down there. And up here, it feels hot. And you?"

"I feel the same thing," she said. "Except not by your throat. It is more in your chest area, fanning up. What area is calling you?"

"Down here," I said, tugging at my t-shirt.

She walked from the foot of the table, reached for her chair, and slid to position herself near the middle of my body. Placing her left hand on my lower abdomen, she scooted her right hand under my lower back.

I caught my breath. "I see a vagina," I said. "It doesn't have any hair on it." A little girl was looking down at her vagina and tentatively poking at it. After a moment, I said, "It's big and swollen. It hurts." The vagina was glued shut. The little girl was curious about the lips that wouldn't open. She knew they belonged to her. It was funny they were called lips. They were only lips if you could move your head sideways like a bird and look at it cockeyed. She tried this.

"How old are you?"

"Between eight and ten."

"Does the little girl want to say anything?"

"Owie, owie, owie."

"It hurts?"

"Yes."

I said to myself, *its okay, Annie. I'm here. You're not alone.*

The energy worker slid her right hand from under my back and suspended it above my vagina. Her left hand stayed anchored on my lower abdomen.

I stopped breathing. *It's okay, Annie. I'm here with you.* The little girl's eyes were wide. Her breathing quickened. I tried to calm her by saying, *She's not going to hurt you. I'm here with you.*

The energy worker's fingers were kneading. She was pulling blocks of jammed-up energy from my body.

The little girl quieted. Grasshoppers were lying on their backs rubbing their tiny feet together. The grasshopper played as if the tiny feet were musical instruments. Then the image moved to a doctor's office. I was with her as she lay on the examining table. I leaned to pull Annie into my arms. *You're very brave, Annie. I love you.*

Annie thought of the energy worker as a doctor and the massage table as an examining table and me as her mom. She was comforted. The doctor would make her all better and her mom was here with her. The doctor was looking deep inside, taking note of the damage. She performed surgery, then bandaged the injury. Annie's lips loosened. The hurt was gone.

Changing positions, the energy worker placed her right hand under my lower back again and her left hand under my head.

I stopped breathing again. "I know what you're doing! I know what you're doing!" My back was up off the table, my hands pushing into the vinyl.

"It's okay, Beth," she said. "It's okay."

"No, it's not! My mother never held me like this!" I lay back on the table and remained stiff. All I wanted to do was sob and be held. "Do you think I'll ever be able to let you hold me while I cry?"

"I don't know, Beth."

"I'm not gonna quit! I'm not gonna give up!"

"Beth, It's okay if you don't ever cry in here."

"But I want to."

CRYSTEL'S LIPS QUIVERED.

I brought the lilacs to my nose. "Mmmmm. Nice." I held out my arms. "Come on, honey. Let Mama help you."

Thankfully, she crawled up. I placed the floppy lilacs on the floor. Her head rested on my chest, her legs sprawled open. This is what a child who hasn't been abused looks like. I kissed her head.

After we rested, Crystel pulled up her shirt, then mine, and glided on my belly like a whale being beached. Skin to skin. It was as if she was connecting our umbilical cords, re-birthing herself, claiming me as her mommy. I didn't say a word. There were no words.

LATELY, JODY HAD BEEN feeling unwanted. After she came home from work, I ran errands. Afterward, she told me how sad she was that the kids never wanted her and that they always asked for me when I was away. "They cry, 'Mama Bef, Mama Bef,'" she said.

She pulled the clothes out of the dryer, dumped them in the basket.

I laughed. Picked up a warm small shirt. "During the day when they get hurt or have a time-out, they cry, 'Mama Joey, Mama Joey.'"

"What about when Antonio doesn't want to drink out of the green—"

"He likes the purple cup. He won't drink from any other."

"You . . . you . . . have to tell me these things!"

"I try to. But there are so many . . ." I picked up another shirt. "These are like doll clothes."

WHEN ANTONIO AND CRYSTEL turned three, I caught sight of Antonio batting the lid of the empty potty chair onto Crissy's hands. Crissy leaned forward from where she was sitting on the couch and lifted the potty lid again.

"No, Cissy!" he hissed. Antonio's eyebrows crunched together. He slapped the lid down again hard on her hands.

"Antonio! Stop that! Right now!" He lifted the lid again. I squeezed his arms, carrying him to his room. I pushed him into his rocker. "You make me so angry, Antonio. Sit there! Don't move! Just sit there!" I squatted and looked into his deep brown eyes. "Don't hurt your sister. Don't ever hurt your sister!" I held tight to his slight frame and forced him to stay in the chair.

The phone rang. "Don't move," I said.

My sister Margaret was on the other end. This time she asked if she and her family could stay with us for a few days. They were visiting from Wisconsin. I had been waiting for this phone call, knowing it would come, knowing what I had to do. I planted myself firmly on the floor. "No." I waited a moment then said, "There isn't any room at the inn." I cringed, waiting to be hit. I recognized my words as one of the hardest things I had ever done, as hard as reporting the sexual abuse, as hard as doing energy work, as hard as breaking old negative patterns. My parents were dead and I was shutting the door on my siblings, one by one. Most importantly, I was breaking a promise I made to my sisters, to always be there for them.

"If you see it that way," my sister said and hung up.

After placing the phone back in its cradle, I returned to Antonio's room, where he was still sitting in the rocker.

"What am I going to do, Antonio, when you don't listen to me?" I picked him up, set him in my lap, and rocked him. "I'm sorry I got so angry. But what should I do when you don't listen to me?"

"Taaa," he said.

"I can't understand what you are saying when you're sucking on your snuggly. What did you say?"

"Taaalk."

I paused. "Should we try a do-over?"

He nodded.

"Let's be quiet, because Crystel is already napping." Walking hand-in-hand to the porch, we sat on the couch. I snuggled him close. We were quiet for a long time. The afternoon heat was baking the sunroom. Our body warmth made me sweat. Antonio's hair was damp. "It's time for a nap, Antonio. Do you want to take my hand or should I carry you?"

"Carry me."

Antonio clamored up my back and threw his arms around my neck.

"The ol' gray mare ain't what she used to be, ain't what she used to be." On "the ain't," I bucked.

He laughed.

In our do-over on the porch, I ignored the slapping of the potty chair. Antonio was tired. I was tired. The potty chair was not the issue. The issue was that Antonio wasn't listening to me when I had asked him several times to come to his room for a nap.

But then I realized there was another issue, my own anger.

More than the children's whining, more than their fighting, my anger bothered me. With thirty years of sobriety, I wanted my anger to be as inaccessible as liquor. We didn't keep alcohol in our home. To drink, I would need to leave our house, drive to a store, walk through the glass doors, choose my beverage, show my license, and hand the clerk money. At any one of these junctures, I could change my mind. My anger was a fuzzy ogre lurking like a spoiled leftover in the refrigerator, unnoticed and forgotten until the drawer was opened and its ugly smell released. I thought back to the fight that I never believed could ever happen.

"MICHAEL, GIVE ME the goddamn key," I said. I was nineteen and Michael was sixteen.

"Fuck you, Ann!"

Thirty keys were on that ring. Michael didn't even have his driver's license, yet he made a hobby of stealing all the keys to make secret copies. I needed the car key to go to town for groceries. I vaulted forward, grabbing him around the waist, forcing him to the ground. His head banged on the hard, dry earth. Grunting, he swung at me with his free hand, stinging my cheek, bringing hot tears to my eyes. I reached for his left hand and the bunched-up keys he clutched. He tried thrusting me off with his right fist, punching any part of my body he could. I used my weight and adrenaline to keep his body matted to the grass.

He fixed on me with stormy blue eyes. "Hit me, Ann! Come on, hit me! Hit me as hard as you can!"

Maybe he thought I wouldn't do it. After all, we had been childhood best friends. I hesitated. Then letting go of him, I hit him as hard, fast, and strong as I could. My fist struck his freckled face, wedging his nose to the side and grinding his head further into the ground. Dead grass stuck in his red hair. Dazed for the moment, Michael dropped the collection of keys from his outstretched hand.

Five younger brothers and sisters were jackals, circling, witnessing our violence. My parents fought. I hated it. I was always so afraid. I didn't want to be the cause of siblings being afraid. Yet, I was.

I looked briefly at the boiling sun. I couldn't remember the last time it had rained.

Michael seized my shirt, ripping it down the front. He left claw marks on my naked skin. I grasped for the keys. Dirt scraped under my fingernails. He latched onto my hair. My skin burned. But I had the keys. I jumped and ran, leaving Michael holding stringy brown strands between his fingers.

Michael got up, then tripped. "You fuckin' bitch, Ann! Give me those keys!"

I took a key off the ring and threw it in the ditch. Fumbling, I got another key loose, pitched it in the tall grass, and staggered up the road.

"Paul, find the key!" Michael said.

My stomach dropped when Paul aligned with Michael and darted into the ditch. Taking another key, I flipped it into the cornfield. Michael chased after me. When he was close, I tossed the rest of the keys into the field. He dashed after them. I gasped for air between sobs. My t-shirt was shredded. I couldn't cover my breasts, no matter how I moved the cloth around. I dipped into the ditch that bordered the cornfield. I walked through rows of corn.

Sitting cross-legged on the ground, under the canopy of green stalks and leaves, I sobbed. That moment I realized I had to leave home. Even with my older brothers no longer at home, I wasn't safe. My best friend was against me. Where could I go? Patrick had moved into Aunt Kate's house after she moved out. Aunt Kate was living with Aunt Myrtle and taking care of her after Aunt Myrtle had a stroke.

Tires spun on gravel. I stood, peeked out of my hiding place. It was Dad's dusty station wagon. I walked home.

"I'm moving out," I announced, opening the front door. "I'm not living here anymore. I'm going to live with Patrick. I can't stay here with Michael!"

Dad crossed, then uncrossed his arms. "Wait until your mother gets home."

"Look at me! Just look at me!" I clutched my tattered shirt. "I can't live here!" I ran to my bedroom to change clothes. Five minutes later, I heard Mother's voice in the kitchen. I told her I was moving out. To my surprise, she didn't argue. She even offered to drive my belongings to the other farm while I followed on my 250 Yamaha.

"Hurry up," she said. "It looks like rain."

The sky had turned grayish. White-gray clouds moved slowly. I took a box from Mother's car, then tossed it onto the grass in front of Aunt Kate's house.

Patrick came outside, letting the screen door bang behind him. "So, I've got a roommate."

There were two bedrooms upstairs. I took the less cluttered, the room closest to the staircase. I cleared a territory for myself and set up my bed. I pushed it below the only window, stacked my t-shirts in one pile on the floor and my jeans next to them, creating a boundary around my bed. Against the wall was a stand-alone brown metal closet. I banged open the doors and it wobbled side to side. I smelled mothballs. I slid Aunt Kate's remaining dresses to one end of the closet.

Patrick's bedroom was off the living room, with a curtain for a divider, only big enough for a single bed and dresser. Aunt Kate had slept there and the windup alarm clock she used still made a loud, clear *tick-tock*. Sitting outside of this room was a black vinyl recliner, on which Patrick was sprawled, watching TV. He smiled.

"Ann, can we fuck?"

I stopped breathing. His legs were thrown over the arms of the recliner. He was touching himself under his dirty gray sweatpants. What was to stop him from asking me every single day? I didn't know why I thought I would be safe here.

Simon raped me even after he got married. David came to my dorm room in college just like he had come into my tent at a family reunion when I was a girl. When would I understand that I was never safe?

The rumbling of thunder was closer. Suddenly, there was a sharp, loud crack. I flinched. "Patrick, I can't. It screws me up psychologically." Someone else was talking, not me.

"Well, you don't mind if I jack off, do you?"

"No." Relief rushed through my body. If it was this easy to stop him, why didn't I say no years ago? I sat kitty-corner from him and kept my eyes fixed on the twelve-inch TV screen. In the background was the *slap, slap, slap* of his hand moving between his legs.

ON DECEMBER 19, 2012, there were three notifications on my phone. Missed calls from Mark, Paul, and Patricia. Immediately, I knew someone had died. These days, I rarely got phone calls from family members, and certainly not three on the same day.

Then David called. Patrick had gone into his bedroom to go on his computer. When he returned, he laid down on the couch. David found him there.

I pictured my morbidly obese brother, thought of our family history of heart disease and his two-pack-a-day habit. Was he watching pornography, jacking off? Then came out to the couch to rest and died of a heart attack?

"My family and I are leaving for Playa del Carmen on Christmas Eve," I said, hoping David would delay the funeral.

He huffed. "Well, we can't hold these things, you know?"

"I can help with the obit."

"Patricia's taking care of that," he said dismissively.

Though Jody had told me that she would support me in canceling our trip to Playa del Carmen, and I knew from research that we would be able to get a refund from the airlines, there was no reason to. My family and I would continue with our holiday plans to have Christmas in Mexico. Twenty years earlier, my dad died the day after Christmas. I went to the funeral home to view his body. I had no desire to see Patrick's dead body. I had seen him naked many times. I was glad he was dead. There was not a chance he could abuse a niece or nephew.

THE OBITUARY IN the *Pierce County Herald* read:

> Patrick enjoyed a great many things in his lifetime. He loved to be a part of the annual hunting camp, playing cards, visiting, being outdoors, watching his trees grow, and being with family. Patrick was a wonderful Uncle to many nieces and nephews. We were all lucky to have him be "Uncle Buck" to our children. He had a kind, loving, and giving nature. He will be greatly missed.

ON THE DAY OF Patrick's funeral, Jody, Antonio, Crystel, and I took a ferry to Cozumel, then a bus ride to The Dolphin Discovery located inside Chankanaab National Park. The park was a conservation area located in the middle of the island, and was created to protect the fauna and flora species of Cozumel. We had come to swim with the dolphins in the turquoise water of the Caribbean Sea. Each of us, taking turns, were raised up above the water surface by two dolphins doing a foot push from the bottom of our feet. Exhilarated, I rose out of the water with my hands held high into the sky.

PART
THREE

PART

THREE

THE FIRST SIGN OF TROUBLE WAS THE GOAT. BUT THANK God for the goat. Jody and I chose Kamp Dels, an hour's drive south from the Twin Cities, for our two toddlers. The petting zoo was a couple of blocks away from our campsite. Sheep, goats, rabbits, llamas, and other animals beckoned Antonio and Crystel. It was the goats that caught their attention the most. The white-and-black goats climbed, rolled balls, and stood on barrels. Jody and I plugged quarters into the feeders for food pellets and showed the children how to feed the goats with a flat, open hand so the animals wouldn't nibble on their fingers. Antonio got anxious and tossed his food at the goats when they got close. I breathed deeply, loving the smell of hay, straw, poop, and animals.

Jody and I took different paths to our campsite. She drove the car with the children while I walked. At the site, she stepped out of our vehicle and lifted Antonio from his car seat.

Crystel's car seat was empty. "Where's Crystel?"

"I thought she was with you," Jody said.

"I thought you had her." Crystel couldn't talk. Her speech was not intelligible. The person who most understood her was Antonio, and he was with us. I pressed my fists to the sides of my head. She could tell no one her first name, her last name, or who her parents were. I spun around, taking in the mass of tents, RVs, trucks, cars, and people. I wanted to scream.

All of us jumped into the vehicle and headed back to where we last remembered being with Crystel. My heart pounded.

Two adults and one boy ran through the petting zoo, past the feathered birds, the calf lying next to her mom, the deer in the shade. All of us spotted Crystel. She was eye to eye with a white, double-bearded goat. They stood in companionable silence, the goat chewing her cud, the little girl waiting for her family to return. My eyes shone and locked on her. I could breathe again. I slowed to a walk, not wanting to scare her.

"Hey, sweetie, here we are," I said. "Good for you for staying put." I gave her a big hug.

Jody kissed her and Antonio gave his sister a tight squeeze. "Cissy, I so scared my heart go out then come back in when I see you."

"We knew just where to find you," I said, giving her a kiss as I buckled her in her car seat.

I WAS LOST UNTIL I was nineteen years old. At age nineteen, I was an inpatient for chemical dependency at Metropolitan Medical Center in the Twin Cities. Aunt Annie, my namesake, my mother's sister, asked me if I would be admitted. She had recently given me her 250 Yamaha motorcycle. Her best friend was the head nurse on the inpatient chemical-dependency floor. I didn't want to go. I didn't belong there. I only drank once in a while. I never had a blackout. But how safe was I, living with Patrick on the dead-end gravel road surrounded by woods? There was no running water; we were showering in the yard at the well pump. A two-hole outhouse was our bathroom. There was no privacy. How long would Patrick tolerate my refusal to be sexual? What was to stop him from raping me? What if he had friends over? No one would be able to hear me scream.

Two weeks later, my parents drove from Wisconsin for a family session at Metropolitan Medical Center. We sat in straight-backed chairs surrounded by the white walls of a small meeting room. There were no windows and only one door. My parents and the counselor faced me. Dad was in a business suit, Mother in a flowery blouse and red lipstick. I dropped my eyes to the floor, slouched, and bounced my knees up and down. "My brothers are having sex with me."

"Who?" my mother asked. She leaned forward, rested her arms on her thighs. Her hair had streaks of gray, and color was rising to her cheeks.

Her question stunned me. Who? Like there could only be one? I skimmed the blank walls of the room. I tilted my head and noticed there was only one light on the ceiling, a square white acrylic fixture. There were no shadows. "All of them," I said.

"How long has this been going on?" she asked, turning toward Dad.

"Years," I said. I clutched my arms to my chest, bent forward and rocked.

My dad crossed and uncrossed his arms, then scuffed his chair back with his feet. The metal legs of his chair scraped at the non-slippery tile. "That's terrible," he said in a gruff voice.

Mother bucked back in her chair. Her eyes were vacant. "We'll talk to the boys."

I rubbed my arms. The counselor had kept her eyes on me the entire time.

My parents left soon after. I went to my room, noticed sunlight coming through the window and shining on my bed. I lay down on my stomach, letting the light land on my back and warm me.

Six hours later, I was called to the nurses station to take a phone call.

"Ann, you're conning everyone," Mother said. "You just want attention." She said the words with such force I could see spittle on her receiver.

I squeezed the phone to my ear, drew it away, and eyeballed the mouthpiece. I brought the phone back to my ear, swept the nurses station with my eyes. In the back room, a nurse was putting pills in small plastic cups. Behind the desk and to the left of me, a petite, short-haired nurse was charting. The faint smell of disinfectant was in the air. I reached to scratch the psoriasis on the small of my back.

"On your pass, come home. Pack all of your belongings, then get out. You're not welcome in our house."

"I'm not lying, Mom." I sagged against the counter. "I'm telling the truth." The nurse stopped charting. I swallowed hard.

Mother was harsh. "You're not a part of this family. We're . . . we're . . . disowning you."

Dad picked up the other line. "Yeah."

"You're out of our will," she said.

The nurse raised her eyebrows. Though the television room was a few feet away, I didn't hear any noise, just the *pound, pound, pound* of my heart. What I feared happening if I ever reported the abuse was happening.

My dad was breathing heavily. "You can't talk to your brothers and sisters until they're eighteen." He cleared his throat. "Make sure you take everything."

I winced. The nurse came around the desk and stood next to me. She was the same height as me. I pressed my free hand to my abdomen and kicked at the floor. She put her hand on my shoulder, steadying me. I was surprised at her strength.

Waiting for my parents' next words, I imagined them arriving home from their two-hour drive—Mother's lipstick fading, Dad's suit rumpled.

"We're done talking," Mother said.

"We're done," Dad echoed.

The nurse took the phone from me and set it in the cradle. She steered me to an open office and asked me to repeat the conversation. Her voice was soft and kind. I waited for a long time before repeating what my parents said. She told me that she was going to have me switch rooms for the night. She wanted me close to the nurses station in case I might want to talk.

I stayed up all night, determined to shed tears. I knew I should cry. But no matter how hard I tried, I couldn't. I was sure something was defective in me, broken, like a clock that quit ticking. You could shake the clock, hear the busted rattle. You knew it wasn't a dead battery. It was something just as essential. And yet, you couldn't find it.

ANTONIO AND CRYSTEL were settling in for the ride home. We waved goodbye to the goats and Kamp Dels.

Jody was driving. She signaled left for the 35W entrance ramp. It was a straight shot home.

I twisted my black Timex. It was ten minutes to noon. We'd be home earlier than planned. The children were watching *Finding Nemo* on our portable DVD player.

Fifteen minutes into the ride, I thought about losing Crystel. I shuddered. "Jody, we can't let this happen again."

Staring straight ahead, she said, "I know." Then she looked at me. "We don't have to wait until Crystel is three to get her tested for speech. There is an agency that will do it right now."

"Give me the number when we get home. I'll call first thing in the morning."

"Let's include Antonio in the testing," Jody said. "We have no idea what's normal, and they'll notice how different Antonio and Crystel are in their speech."

One month later, the results stated that there wasn't anything defective with their speech. Any delays were due to the children having been adopted as infants. Of course, this didn't explain why we could understand Antonio better than Crystel. Jody and I were more than happy to wait for Crystel to catch up to her peers.

That fall, we enrolled the children in a Spanish immersion preschool two days a week. Antonio's class was in the morning, Crystel's in the afternoon. One day before school, Crystel asked me to braid her hair. I could have bunched up her hair and wrapped a rubber band around the mound, but she wanted a braid. "Crystel, why don't you pick up your dollhouse and I'll be back." Earlier, we sat cross-legged on the floor and had a family dinner with two moms and a baby. As she took the pretend food off the reddish-brown barbecue grill, the baby boy started crying. I rocked him in my palm to quiet him. I swished away thoughts of how I hated the dollhouse my mother gave me when I was eight. I wanted to be outside playing with my brothers.

Fishtail braid, French braid, French Over, French Rope, Princess Ann Braid, Rope Braid. I was Googling how to braid a little girl's hair. I just wanted a basic braid. *Separate the pony-tail into three equal strands. Hold two strands in your right hand with your palm facing up. Hold the third strand in your left hand. Turn your right hand over so your palm is now facing down.* I touched my fingertip to my lips and studied the picture.

Separating Crystel's hair into three parts, I started weaving the strands. My mind was on her garbled speech and the last conversation I had with her preschool teacher. "Crystel should be speaking clearer. I can't understand her."

"But we had her tested and she passed. We were told that it would just take time," I had argued.

"Have her tested again." She handed me a white envelope. "Inside are Hennepin County resources, with phone numbers."

I paused, held Crystel's hair taut. How did this go? Crossing the right and left sections over the middle, I continued weaving until I ran out of hair. Why didn't we do more the first time she was tested? Why didn't we get a second opinion? I answered my own question: Because we wanted her to be all right. I stared at Crystel's braid. Once I came upon Crystel and Antonio in the bathroom. She was sitting on a stool. He was carefully taking the snarls out of her hair with a doll comb. After straightening her hair, he bundled it into a pony-tail. He probably did a better job than me, I mused.

"Okay, Crystel." I tied a band around the ends of her hair. "I am all done." I felt in my pants pocket for the slip of paper with the phone numbers. "Would you like a ribbon, too?"

As we drove down Penn Avenue to Crystel's school, I saw a mom pushing a stroller on the sidewalk and a boy running ahead of her. Jody and I thought we were doing right by allowing Crystel to grow into her words. Yet what we lost was precious time.

Every day, Antonio decoded Crystel's speech for us. On the playground, he regularly held a place for her at the top of the slide, causing a jam-up of children. When she was sitting next to him, they slid to the bottom. At night, he slept with a blanket filled with stars and moons. Before saying goodnight the evening before, he had drawn my attention to a sliver of a moon and said, "That's C for Cissy."

"You get to sleep with her, then, don't you?" I said.

He smiled, happy I understood.

BECAUSE MICHAEL WAS my favorite brother growing up, I used to spend so much of my day with him that my mother eventually admonished me. "Paul doesn't have anyone to play with," she said, pushing me toward my other siblings.

Michael and I had a long history. After chemical dependency treatment, I moved into a halfway house. Now, it was Michael who was in treatment. In my family, it was acceptable—even expected—to be chemically dependent. After I was forbidden to talk to my siblings, I called Michael and asked to meet with him and his counselor. I wanted to tell the counselors about our family. I wanted us both to get help.

The room was stark. Michael sat on a worn brown couch. His counselor sat in a folding chair that had been carried in. I took the remaining chair next to an end table. *Twenty-Four Hours a Day*, a little black book, sat on the bottom shelf.

Eventually Michael admitted bypassing me, having sex instead with two younger sisters. He told me he didn't understand his feelings, why he was compelled to be sexual. He thought he was crazy. He was remorseful. He was in his late teens then.

"If I could have had sex with you, I would have," he said.

I remember how the warmth left my outer extremities at his words, how I wiggled my toes, my fingers. How I reached over my shoulder to scratch my suddenly itching back. I picked up the little black book, rifled through it, put it back.

"You were my favorite brother because you never asked me for sex," I told him after a few minutes. "I was safe with you."

But all along, Paul and Michael were assaulting my sisters inside the base of the empty silo. They set it up in a similar way to how the incest began between me and my four older brothers, when I was eight. A game, someone's caught with no escape.

Chills ran through me.

"I'm thinking that Mark is having sex with Catherine," he added.

I thought about the abortion I had when I was fourteen and the baby I had when I was seventeen.

The next day, I met with an attorney to press charges against my brothers. I had to keep my sisters safe. My parents had already told me that they didn't believe me. I knew what would happen if I did nothing. There would be more pregnancies. There would be more abortions. There would be more babies put up for adoption. The attorney explained the most effective action would be to report the sexual abuse. She gave me a referral to a hospital that would conduct an intake interview, then send my statement to social services in Wisconsin.

I met with an intake counselor at Fairview–Southdale Hospital. After I recounted the abuse, I asked for a copy of the

letter that she would send to Ellsworth. I wanted proof that I
reported the incest, that I tried to stop my brothers.

November 7, 1978

Dale Langer
Pierce County Social Services 7 P.O. Box 183
Ellsworth, Wisconsin

Dear Mr. Langer,

On November 1, 1978, I conducted an intake interview with Ann Smith, a twenty-year-old single, white
female, from a family of twelve children, currently in
residence at Crossroads Halfway House. [. . .] Ms. Smith
had been referred to me by Ms. M. Michaels, an attorney
whom she had consulted for a legal opinion.

Ms. Smith informed she was looking for therapy for
herself because she had been incestuous from around
age six or seven until May 1978 with seven of her brothers, who presently range in age from fifteen to twenty-
four. [. . .] She estimated about one time every two weeks
with some one of her brothers. She stated the sexual activity consisted of intercourse and/or oral sex. She further stated that she informed her parents . . . and said
her parents said it's good you told us, but they have
taken no action on the problem.

In September of 1978, Ms. Smith's brother, Michael,
age seventeen, was in the adolescent chemical dependency treatment program. [. . .] While there he informed
his parents that he had been sexual with his younger sisters, saying he had approached his sister, Catherine, age
fourteen, and when she refused, he bypassed her and

was sexual three months ago with Margaret, twelve, and Patricia, eleven. Ms. Smith said the above sexual activities occurred at the Smith home. . . .

Ms. Smith stated that since that time her father told her the incest had stopped and that "everybody is okay."

[. . .] I consulted with Debbie Anderson, Hennepin County Attorney's Office, and she informed me that Wisconsin law does not require that sexual abuse be reported but that it may be.

[. . .] I would appreciate receiving an acknowledgement of this report, and a follow-up report on the action taken.

Thank you for your help.
Sincerely,
Maureen A. Kramlinger
Intake Counselor
Family Sexual Abuse Program

Cc: Ann Smith

"WE'RE HERE, CRYSTEL." I parked in front of Joyce United Methodist Church in the Uptown neighborhood of Minneapolis. The Spanish immersion preschool was in the basement of the church. "Let's go see your best friend."

I carried Crystel to the front door, set her down, and took her hand. Walking down the stairs, we kept our eyes open for Antonio.

Antonio came running. First, he gave Crystel a big hug, then jumped up into my arms. "*Oooof.* You're my boy, Antonio." I squeezed him tight.

A FEW WEEKS LATER, Crystel was tested by our school district. They diagnosed Crystel with articulation disorder. Her brain knew what it wanted to say, but the sound didn't travel to her mouth. Crystel started morning speech classes twice a week in our school district.

AT 8:15 IN THE MORNING, Antonio and I waited with Crystel until her bus came.

"Your small-like-a-mouse bus is going to be here any second," Antonio said. He raced out the door to the bus. "Come on, Cissy."

Crystel promenaded behind Antonio. Mardi Gras beads from her headband dangled down her back. Her one blue sock and one white sock matched the daisies on her skirt. Antonio bounced up the bus steps.

"What seat do you want, Cissy?" he asked.

She chose the second to last seat on the right. I followed behind her, carrying her backpack. Antonio reached for her seatbelt, pulled it across her waist. Her small stature hit me like a fist in my stomach. I almost crumpled. *She's only three, for God's sakes. I was younger than her when I was first touched.*

"You were two years old when I saw David touching you," Mother said. She laughed. "He was only four. How would he know such a thing?"

My first memory was when I was four. It was in our cellar, spooky, eerie, and heart-stopping.

Dim yellow light glowed from a bare bulb. The floor was dirt, smelled of earth. The outside cellar doors never opened. The potato bin was empty most of the time. Things were to be discovered down there. A black potbelly stove with a missing foot leaned against the flaky white cement wall. A dusty hot-chocolate machine with a cut cord sat on a long wooden plank table. Canning jars in all shapes and sizes ranged along the walls. The cellar was alive with cobwebs and little voices.

"Come on! Come on, bring your pennies here," barked Simon, my red-headed oldest brother, with the spirit of an eight-year-old. He stood behind lined-up pop bottles and held golden jar rings. "Ring a bottle and win a prize," he hollered. Seven-year-old Patrick matched his tone and sung, "Drop your pennies here, folks. Right here. Stand directly above the jar and drop it in. An easy win. Easy win. This nice teddy bear could be yours. Step right up. Hurry now!"

Two other brothers were talking amongst themselves.

I scuffled around the cellar, wide-eyed, pennies squeezed tight in my four-year-old fist.

"Hey, Ann, come here." Simon's red head poked up from the potato bin.

"What?"

"Come here, over here."

Leaving the chatter of brothers in the background, I shuffled over to the bin and climbed in. It was the size of a coffin. Simon squirmed and moved. Suddenly, I was under him. I kept my feet from touching the sides and any runaway potatoes, usually squishy and gray, stuck between the boards. He pulled his shorts down, then mine. Moving up and down, his chest pushed into my trunk. I couldn't breathe. I couldn't see. My chest hurt.

"Don't tell Mom," he said, climbing off me.

The pennies that were so tight in my fist had fallen out of my hand. I left them scattered in the dark and crept upstairs to the kitchen light.

ANTONIO FASTENED CRYSTEL'S SEATBELT. "There you go, Cissy," he said. She lost her grip on her new, not-yet-sharpened pencil, a Halloween pencil topped with a large blue ghost eraser. It fell to the floor of the bus and rolled under her seat. Antonio retrieved it for her.

"Tanks, Toe (thanks, Antonio)," she said. Her eyes shone bright at her brother.

She tugged my shirt. "Bye, Mum-Mum. Can I tell you sumpan?" she asked.

"Sure, honey." I leaned over and gave her a kiss on the cheek.

"Ill you ave at me? (will you wave at me?)"

"Antonio and I will both wave at you."

A WEEK LATER, I was picking up Crystel at speech school. I lifted her into my arms and gave her a kiss.

"Not go Toe school," she announced. "Only iss (this) school."

I shortened my steps to our car. "Really?" Her face was serious. "Which school do you want to go to, Victoria or Morgan's?" Victoria's was the Spanish immersion preschool and Morgan's was her speech school.

"Mogan, iss school."

"You don't want to go to Alejandra's school?" Alejandra was Crystel's new friend who also attended afternoon Spanish immersion preschool.

"Iss school."

"I'll talk with Mama Jody."

"I wauve you, Mum-Mum," she said. Stretching out her arms, she hugged my neck and kissed me on the cheek.

Driving away from speech school, I looked at my watch. Jody wouldn't be home for another five hours. I reached under the seat for my cell phone, tried to call her. She didn't answer, so I left a message. Sometimes it was better if I didn't speak directly to Jody. She'd need the full five hours until I saw her to process the idea. I had to pretend that I hadn't already made up my mind.

Leaves had fallen off trees, carpeting lawns in orange and red. Some homes had thirty-two-gallon pumpkin lawn bags scattered around their house and yard. What do introverted people do with all the unprocessed information floating in their head? Was it like having buoys in their mind? Did they have so many things to mull over that these buoys needed to be separate colors or at separate depths in their brain? What happened to the buoys after the introverted person made a decision? Did they sink to the bottom of the ocean, another buoy popping up to take its place?

Naked trees towered over the landscape. I shivered. "Are you cold, Crissy?" I said to her in the back seat.

"No, Mama. I hot."

"What did you do in school today, colors, numbers, or words?"

"I counted to a hundred today." She started to sing, and even though her words were jumbled, I knew the song. "There were ten in the bed and the little one said, 'Roll over! Roll over!' So they all rolled over and one fell out."

I turned onto the freeway while Crystel sang, "Ten in the bed." How many times was I raped? The numbers were in the November 7, 1978, letter, and the math was not complicated.

Born in 1958, seven years old in 1965, rapes stopped in 1978. That would be thirteen years, once every two weeks. Twenty-six times a year for thirteen years is three hundred and thirty-eight times. That's an approximate. It certainly wasn't any less.

A person learned a lot when they had done something three hundred and thirty-eight times. "Oooooooooo! Splat!" My daughter sang. "Then there was just one in the bed!" Think how accomplished you would be after parachuting, flying a plane, driving a racecar, putting out forest fires, or selling real estate after three hundred and thirty-eight times. "And the little one said, 'Hey! Where did everybody go! Mom! I want to sleep in your bed!'"

You probably would call yourself an expert.

I pulled to the curb of the brick church. "We're here, Crystel." I unbuckled her. We walked hand in hand into the mammoth building. At the bottom of the basement steps, her friend Alejandra, an adopted girl from Columbia, rushed to Crystel. She stood directly in front of her and said, "Hi." Alejandra's curly dark hair flowed down to her shoulders. Today, she had a blue bow clasped in her hair. Crystel gave Alejandra a little smile. Alejandra took her hand.

Later that evening, after the children were in bed, Jody and I agreed that Crystel only needed to attend speech school. In an effort to preserve Crystel's friendship with Alejandra, I set up a playdate for Crystel at her house for the coming Saturday.

On the way home from her playdate with Alejandra, Crystel said, "Alejandra has mum, dad, bra (brother) name José." She pointed to Jody in the driver's seat, "I have a mum." She pointed to me, "and a mum." She pointed to Antonio, "and a bra, Toe."

Tears formed in the corner of my eyes. I squeezed Jody's hand, then reached back and touched Crystel's and Antonio's legs. "We need to celebrate," I said, as a comfortable warmth rose on my face.

"DQ," Antonio hollered.

"Let's see who can eye spy it first."

"There it is. There it is," Antonio said.

In the restaurant, there were two rows of booths. Antonio chose a booth for his family. Packed together eating icecream, we were a family, the four of us. We belonged to each other.

Crystel licked her vanilla ice-cream cone slowly and told Antonio about her playdate. Her words were garbled. I deduced that she and Alejandra played with fuzzy little rabbits that wore diapers and that Crystel wanted a rabbit, too. Antonio asked if they were toy bunnies. Crystel nodded.

My Peanut Buster Parfait was just the right amount of hot fudge and crunchy peanuts, a great salt-and-sugar combo, the best of both worlds. "It's nice that you're friends," I said. I leaned over the table, looked from one to the other. "I want you to always have each other. You're family."

IN DECEMBER 1978, THE FINAL schism in my farm family occurred when I accompanied Mrs. Smook, a social worker assigned to investigate my allegations of abuse, to Ellsworth. Mrs. Smook was the social worker who placed my baby for adoption in 1975. She had legal access to Margaret, Patricia, and John, who were grade-school students at St. Francis School. Mother and Dad couldn't keep me from seeing my siblings. They were also unaware that we were making this visit to the school.

Blonde-haired eleven-year-old Margaret followed a nun up the flight of stairs to her office. I stood when Margaret walked into the room. She looked at Mrs. Smook. She looked at me. She crossed her pale arms, her fingernails digging into her skin. "You aren't my sister. I don't know you!" she screamed. She marched out of the room.

I dropped to the couch, held my hands in my lap. The nun gathered her black holy habit and left. Mrs. Smook sat in a large, gray, overstuffed chair. Books, papers, and unopened mail were piled on a desk. Rubber boots and an umbrella leaned in a corner. Dust bunnies and small paper clippings lay about on the dull green carpet. *This was the room,* I said to myself. I was eight when two nuns shut the door and asked me to take off my dress. I did as I was told. Worn, thin underwear hugged my slim hips. "Turn around," one of them said. They were pointing to the scaly patches on my body. The next day my mother took me to Dr. Klaas. He recommended my mother to a dermatologist in the Twin Cities for my just-diagnosed psoriasis.

I turned toward Mrs. Smook. "Margaret used to bang her head against the wall when she was two and three years old. Sometimes it was the floor." I sniffled, taking a Kleenex from the box on the desk. "I thought she'd crack her head open."

The nun returned with Patricia and John, who were more willing to talk with us. Patricia and John both said that things were fine at home. I looked them over from head to toe. They seemed all right. They didn't have any marks or bruises on them. They looked fed. Their clothes were clean. "No one died. You always had enough to eat," I remembered my parents saying. As if that was the be-all and end-all. But now, I didn't have anything else to go by, either.

Mrs. Smook and I drove a block to the middle school to meet with Catherine, then on to the homestead, where Patrick still lived and Michael had just moved in after getting out of chemical dependency treatment. They both confirmed that the incest had stopped.

Our final meeting was with Paul. It was now his turn at a chemical dependency treatment facility, the same facility Michael had been in.

I asked Mrs. Smook to send me a copy of her investigation.

December 26, 1978

Mrs. Maureen A. Kramlinger
Intake Counselor
Family Renewal Center
Fairview-Southdale Hospital
Minneapolis, MN

SUBJECT: Ms. Ann Smith

Dear Ms. Kramlinger:

This letter is to acknowledge the referral you made on Ann Smith's behalf, regarding the incest between herself and her siblings, to the Pierce County, Department of Social Services . . . on 11-7-78. On 12-1-78, Mr. Dale Langer . . . requested our department to follow up on it as Ann's father . . . works for the Unified Services Board and works closely with the County Department and Ann's mother . . . has been employed by their Department as a social worker.

[. . .] I met with Ann and she accompanied me to Ellsworth on 12-12-78. I filed a report with our Child Abuse Registry on 12-13-78 on the three minor girls residing in the Smith home. [. . .]

I believe I am accurate when I state that Ann and I drew similar conclusions about the incest. The girls and Michael and Paul verified their parent's contention that the incest has ceased as of approximately July '78 for them and the girls do not seem particularly upset about those experiences. [. . .]

This does not mean there are not a lot of family problems, but our concern turned to helping Catherine, age fourteen, to deal with the family patterns. Catherine is very unhappy and was asking for placement in a foster home as she felt she is unable to cope with the stress the parents, in particular, had laid on her to "be good" and be a surrogate mother while ostracizing her from their care and concern.

After finally reaching both parents on 12-14-78 by phone (they were always busy) and the ensuing discussions, I could appreciate the tentative conclusion I reached [. . .] that it is going to be nearly impossible to get the parents into family therapy and the only hope for the children is to leave the home and seek help on their own.

[. . .] Although things are still "up in the air," I will follow it out. I was impressed with the individual strength I saw in all the Smith children and the warm feelings between the siblings. Ann appears to be dealing with herself quite well and I believe it was helpful just for her to talk with them.

Thank you for your interest in this matter, as it probably wouldn't have "come to light" otherwise and now we have something specific to deal with.

Sincerely,

Barbara Smook

Adoption and Permanent Planning Section Division of Community Services Western Regional Office

Cc: Ann Smith

"Mama Bef," Antonio said. He was fanning himself, sitting across from me at DQ.

"Yes, hon?" I licked the hot fudge off my spoon.

"You're staring at people again."

Once school let out for the summer, Jody and I enrolled Crystel in private speech therapy. I was assigned daily homework. After dinner, Crystel and I went to her bedroom and sat in her rocker. I picked up a folder filled with pictures. I pulled a photo out, she named it. I picked the next photo up, and we rifled through the stack. Even with a picture, I didn't understand anything she was saying. I gave up. I stopped doing the homework.

One afternoon, her speech pathologist said, "Crystel's the hardest worker I have. She always does her best. Are you doing her homework?"

That evening we started again. With Crystel in my lap, I pointed to a picture of fire.

"Ire," Crystel said.

I moved my finger to a firefighter.

"Ireighter."

To a shark's fin.

"In."

At our next appointment, I asked the speech pathologist if Crystel would be like this forever. I gently bit my lip.

"I have never worked with anyone past seven or eight years old," she replied.

This gave me hope. I was her mother. I shouldn't give up, no matter how impossible it seemed. Crystel never gave up on herself.

THAT FALL, MONDAY, September 11, 2006, Morgan, her school teacher, wanted to speak with me in private.

"Crystel is four, returning to the same classroom, and she should be more socially active," she said. "We should have her tested for autism."

"Oh," I said in an agreeable voice. I stared at my empty hands and wanted to fall to the floor. I was devastated not that Crystel might be autistic but that it wasn't me who raised the concern. Like a dog that studied his master, I scrutinized Antonio's and Crystel's every vocalization and gesture and adjusted my parenting to what I saw. I had learned their habits, mannerisms, and movements.

Jody and I regularly responded to any problems with the children before they became more marked. After the infants were born, we sent a videotape of them to the University of Minnesota International Adoption Clinic for a pre-adoption medical review. Growth, development, and any long-term risks for signs of alcohol or other prenatal exposures were evaluated. After they came home, we followed up with a post-adoption physical examination, initial development status, and laboratory evaluation. Doctor visits continued until all our questions and concerns were answered. Always, we stayed on top of their needs. If Crystel were autistic, how did I not know this and raise the flag myself?

Crystel was playing quietly in the corner of the classroom with a dollhouse. I walked over and took her hand.

"Come here, honey." I lifted her into my arms and gave her a kiss on the cheek. My eyes were hot. I had let my little girl down.

Once we were in the car, I glanced in the back seat. Crystel wasn't buckled in.

"Tat's (that's) okay, Mum-Mum. I ooo (do) it."

I shook my head and waved my hand in front of me.

"Ooo okay, Mum-Mum?"

"Yes, honey." But the doubts were lingering in my mind. Specialists had evaluated Crystel at two and a half years old; they said not speaking was normal. Jody and I questioned their diagnosis. Morgan, her school speech teacher, didn't offer the suggestion of private speech therapy until I had asked. Crystel would have fallen even further behind in her speech development over the summer. Having the family I grew up in also made me question so-called "experts." My mother was a social worker, my father a chemical dependency counselor. They were professionals in their field, yet I suffered sexual abuse and our family life was anything but normal.

Crystel was singing in the backseat.

I whispered into the phone, "Jody, I'm with Antonio and Crystel every single day. Wouldn't I know if she was autistic? Wouldn't you know?" We discussed Crystel's chosen aunts. Aunt Pat was a school psychologist, and as part of her job, she tested for autism. Aunt Ann was an elementary school social worker. Certainly they would have mentioned autism.

"Call her speech pathologist," Jody said. "She knows her better than Morgan."

As soon as I parked in our driveway, I hurried Crystel inside and set her up with a snack.

"Mum-Mum?"

"Yes, Crystel?"

"You ave me ittle ishies (you gave me little fishies). I ate ittle ishies (I hate little fishies)." She rubbed the back of her neck.

I stopped. "You are right, honey. Those are for Antonio. Just a moment." I poured Honey Nut Cheerios in a bowl for her, added milk. "How's this?"

She smiled.

I walked quickly to the phone, dialed her speech pathologist. "The school wants to test Crystel for autism," I said.

She took an audible breath. "I have not seen any signs of autism from Crystel," she said. "She is still learning speech and is extremely shy. Though I can't tell you what to do, I would advise you not to have Crystel tested. I don't see the signs."

I interrupted her. "I'm afraid that if they test Crystel their findings will be positive and it will go on her school record, which will affect her all of her life and . . . and . . ." I stopped talking.

The pathologist began to tell me stories of children that she had treated successfully.

IN HIGH SCHOOL, I overheard the guidance counselor telling the vocational rehab counselor that I'd never make it through college. But he didn't know me, really know me. Couldn't that be the same as the teacher wanting to test Crystel for autism? She didn't really know or understand Crystel.

IN MAY 1976, I GRADUATED near the bottom of my class of one hundred and thirty kids. I never got my picture in the yearbook, never went to a prom, was kicked out of school the last week, and wrongfully accused of throwing water balloons. I was forbidden on the senior boat ride down the St. Croix River. But I graduated.

Applying to the University of Wisconsin–Stout was the thing to do after I was rejected from the Navy for my psoriasis.

My first week at Stout, I walked into the career guidance office and asked the advisor to give me every test he could.

His ponytail was tied back; he had earrings in both ears. He asked me why. I explained that I overheard my high school counselor talking about me. "She'll flunk out the first semester." I was desperate to know the truth. Was I stupid, mentally retarded, or a psycho?

A week later, he laid the results in front of me: intelligence, inkblot, and personality tests. He said I might need a little help in math, but I'd do all right.

At the end of my first semester, I earned a 3.5 grade point average and received a Chancellor's award.

That was a year before I reported the abuse, before being kicked out of the house. During holiday break, my mother found me in my bedroom, scissors in hand. Newspaper clippings, stacks of the weekly *Herald*, envelopes, and stamps were scattered on the bed.

"Ann, what are you doing?"

"I'm sending the announcement of my Chancellor's award to all those teachers who said I wouldn't make it."

"I wish you didn't have to do that," she said, shaking her head. "Can I have a stamp to mail in our income tax forms?"

"Are you claiming me as a tax deduction?"

"Yes, I am. Why?"

"Then you owe me six hundred dollars. It says right on the tax form that you have to give your dependent at least six hundred dollars in support to claim them. I'm not getting anything from you. Maybe I would get more scholarship money if you didn't claim me."

My mother walked away, shutting the door behind her.

I HELD THE PHONE to my ear. The speech pathologist had just finished explaining further speech treatment available for Crystel.

"Maybe Jody and I can create more social situations for her without Antonio around," I said. "Antonio has such a big personality. Maybe he's taking too good of care of her, not letting her speak?" Maybe he thought he was saving her?

She agreed. We hung up.

WHEN I REPORTED the incest to the authorities, I did it to save my sisters. I didn't realize it would affect nieces and nephews until my brother Thomas, who hardly ever spoke, called me four years after I reported the abuse. Funny thing—despite being disowned, I was never entirely in or out of the family.

"Ann, would you come talk to us? They won't let me adopt Molly." Thomas paused. Molly was four years old, his wife's child from a previous relationship. "If you talk to the social worker, tell them I'll be a good father . . ."

I drove to Wisconsin, to their trailer on the homestead. It was late September, a cold, windy day. Thomas's wife sat next to him on the couch. The trailer became smaller and smaller with each word I spoke. Frigid air seeped in through the joists. The walls were cascading in on us. Thomas's memory couldn't be jogged even though I helped with the details, such as the car ride home when I gave him a blowjob, such as the hideout above the milk house, such as the crawl space in our old house, such as the back of the pickup on our way to Apple River. I was uncomfortable talking in front of his wife but he insisted that he couldn't remember. He sounded earnest. I tried hard to help him remember.

Finally, I said, "I'll make an appointment to talk with your social worker." I believed that he would make a good father.

Even so, Thomas wasn't allowed to adopt.

His wife was furious. "What did you tell 'em?" She wanted me to recant my statements and tell them that I made the abuse up.

"I told them that Thomas would make a good father. It wasn't my decision he couldn't adopt, it was the judge's," I said.

"Ann, you just want attention! It isn't even true! I'll call a family meeting and—"

"And do what?" I demanded. "Bring it into the light?" I stood taller. A judge was keeping others safe now.

She never called the meeting. She quit speaking to me for years.

AFTER THE CHILDREN went to bed that evening, Jody and I discussed how we could provide Crystel with more situations that were social. We enrolled her in two additional half-mornings of preschool and I organized and started a weekly playgroup with her classmates. The playgroup rotated to a new house every week.

A couple months later, Morgan asked again to test Crystel. She also wanted to observe her in the new preschool setting we had arranged. An expert on autism would observe with her. She insisted that early detection was imperative in treating an autistic child.

"Let me talk to Jody," I said.

Jody and I discussed the pros and cons of allowing Crystel to be tested. We also called their aunts, who were both professionals. Both of them said not to have her tested. The teacher didn't know Crystel like we did and we were right, they said, she would be labeled.

I knew about labels. I attended my five-year and ten-year school reunions. I wanted people to see me differently from the label I had in high school. I overheard a friend saying, "She's not like that anymore." After my ten-year reunion, realizing that I would always be the slut who had a baby, I never attended another.

Crystel's teacher didn't know how extremely shy she was. Children who are shy are not very talkative and often look down or away when someone else talks to them. They also spend a lot of the time by themselves. Still, they do talk to people some of the time, especially to family members and friends with whom they are comfortable, and they like to be around people some of the time. Children with autism may appear to be shy, but shyness and autism are very different from each other. The symptoms of autism can range from mild to severe. Children with the most extreme forms of autism are almost totally isolated socially. Lacking the ability to relate normally to others, they prefer to be alone. Even within their own family, they seldom make eye contact or try to share their interests in toys or other objects. Many children with autism never learn to talk at all. In contrast, Crystel enjoyed being with her family, her aunts and uncles, neighbors, and her neighbor friend. She laughed, talked, and played jokes on them. Already, her dry and intelligent sense of humor was being seen. We often accompanied her across the street to visit her friend, only leaving when the two girls were heard chattering in her bedroom. It was also true that when the doorbell rang she ran and hid. But so did Antonio.

"No," I simply said the next day when I met with Morgan. "You don't have our permission to test or observe Crystel other than in your own classroom."

AFTER MY VISIT WITH Thomas, Michael's wife, Terri, called. "Ann, was there physical abuse in your family?" she asked. "Michael and I are meeting with a counselor. He pushed me the other day. Is this a one-time thing or might it get worse?"

I took a deep breath. "There was a lot of physical abuse in my family. Brothers hitting brothers, parents hitting each other, brothers hitting sisters, brothers hitting Dad."

In the space before she asked the next question, I recalled the time I stood with my hand on the phone at the farmhouse ready to call the police. Mother whacked Dad on his back with a broomstick until it broke. He pushed her to the wall, pinning her.

"What else?" Michael's wife asked. "What did Michael do?"

Snow covered the pool cover. I scanned over it as I said, "Michael hit our mother. He was seventeen. I told him to stop hitting her, to leave her alone. I don't know if he ever did it again."

"Okay," she sighed. "We've been having trouble for a while and his pushing me was the last straw. I told Michael I was going to call you and he said that he didn't care."

I hung up the phone. Heavier snow was falling now.

WHEN SPRING ARRIVED, Antonio, Crystel, and I got into the routine of hollering when we spotted Christmas wreaths. On the way to preschool one day, I said, "There's a wreath on that . . . that . . . that thing."

"That's a fence, Mom," Crystel said.

I thought, *ire fire, ireighter firefighter, FENCE.* She found her F! I wanted to stop the car and scream, "She found her F!"

ON THE WEEKENDS, Jody yelled, "Okay, breakfast is ready!" Pancakes, sausage, bacon, and hashbrowns were set out on the table. One morning, Crystel said something that I didn't catch. "What, Crystel?"

"Cissy would like sausage," Antonio said.

"No, Toe. No sausage. I want pancakes and bacon."

Crystel would no longer allow Antonio to speak for her.

LATE SPRING, AT CRYSTEL'S last school consultation of the year, I argued with myself. Still, I had to know. "Morgan, do you still think Crystel might be autistic?" I asked.

"No," she answered. "Crystel watches out for others in the classroom. She tries to include them in her play."

Yes. I wanted to pump my fist in the air. I locked my eyes on Crystel and smiled.

On the drive home, I noticed that the flowers on the shadow side of houses were starting to bloom.

ANOTHER BROTHER CALLED. Loyal Paul warned me not to tell his two teenage daughters about the sexual abuse and harm their relationships with our brothers. "Patrick is their favorite uncle," he said, "and it's because of you that Simon doesn't have a relationship with his kids. And by the way, Margaret burnt the children's books you sent her."

"*Good Touch, Bad To—*" I tried to explain.

"Don't. Ever. Bring up the abuse."

I thought about Mrs. Smook's words. *I appreciate the tentative conclusion I reached—that it is going to be nearly impossible to get the parents into family therapy and the only hope for the children is to leave home and seek help on their own.*

"My brothers are my friends," Paul added.

I hung up the phone. Two beds of flowers circled our backyard. In the shadowy light, I could make out their blossoms. I'd be there for anyone who called.

MY NIECE, TINA, CALLED. She was nineteen and had just reported Simon to the police for being violent with her brother, Simon's son. Tina was Simon's oldest daughter. She was twelve when her mother died. When she was fourteen, before I left for the Peace Corps, I told her about the sexual abuse and that I had a son her age.

I called the number she gave me and sent her social worker a copy of the 1978 police report.

Years later, she asked me to walk her down the aisle.

Saturday, June 2, 2001, Simon, Tina, and I stood side by side inside the entrance of the Church of Saint Joseph.

"You're not really going to cry, are you?" Simon asked.

I held a wet glob of Kleenex. "I'm already crying."

Simon grimaced. Shuffled his feet. He turned to face his daughter. "Tina, are you going to let me kiss you at the altar?" he asked gruffly. His tone was demanding.

"No," she said.

I straightened, leaned slightly forward to look at them. His right arm was linked in hers. I raised my eyebrows, waiting for his reaction. The Catholic church rang with the sound of the piped music and smelled fragrant with the wildflowers held in bouquets by bridesmaids and pinned on tuxedos and dresses. The stained-glass windows lit up with colors and figures intermittently as the sun pushed clouds out of the way for moments at a time. Candles shone on the altar, glowing, beckoning.

Simon and Tina's mother were married at this same altar twenty-seven years earlier. I was a bridesmaid then, in a light blue gown. Thirteen years after their wedding, I stood at the lectern reading to the congregation, "For everything there is a season . . ." as Tina's mom lay in a casket.

Simon was careful not to bump Tina's veil. "I'm proud of you. You look nice."

I dabbed at my eyes. "Yeah, me too."

Simon frowned at me.

I frowned back. "It's your daughter's wedding. It's okay to cry." I looked down the aisle at the altar and thought of Tina's mother. I couldn't stop the tears.

"Annnn," Simon warned. His face tensed, snarling. My mother always said that Simon and I were the only ones who snarled: our left lips squinched up, forcing skin to touch the nose, teeth bared.

"Sssssssh," I said. "Sssssssh," I looked forward, tears streaming down my face, worried Tina would have no good pictures of her walk down the aisle.

Later, when it came time for family portraits, Simon nudged me. "Come on, Ann. They want all of us."

"No, they want the parents. You're her parent."

"You're standing in for her mother," he said with steel in his voice.

"No, I'm not. I'm her aunt."

"They want you up there."

"No. I'm her aunt. I'm not her mom."

Tina, her sister, and two brothers, stood at the altar waiting. A shudder ran through me as I pictured a family portrait with Simon and me encircling his children. I saw the photograph on a fireplace mantle and it felt all wrong. It was just too close to the truth. A brother and sister having children.

"No, I'm not. I'm standing in for me. I'm her aunt," I said adamantly. I pushed my back into the pew.

"Goddamn it, oh, all right," he said as he left the pew to join his children.

Watching them gather as a family of five, Simon and his four children, gave me time to understand how he made sense of all this. I realized that in his mind I was standing in for his dead wife, or Tina's mom, and not as a special person with a relationship with his daughter.

I recalled the day after his wife died of cancer. I drove an hour to his house. I wanted to be of help. No one was home but him.

"Come with me to the house I own," he said. "I need to fix the plumbing."

"Sure." I reached for the door handle and slid into the front seat of his station wagon.

He backed out of the driveway.

As soon as we were on the street, I started to lose my breath. I couldn't take my hand off of the door handle. This feeling was the same as when he asked me on a winter day to ride up to Aunt Kate's with him. I was sixteen and he was twenty. He had asked in front of Mother. He was married. I was sure that I was safe. A half mile from Aunt Kate's, he pulled over at the cemetery gates. "People think I'm divorcing her anyway," he said.

I couldn't stop thinking about what was going to happen when we got to that house. Would anyone be there? Simon chatted pleasantly. Every cell in my body lit up. What would I do or say if he reached for me after we got into the house? My breathing was short, rapid. It was then I realized that when my brothers felt stress, I was raped, and wouldn't he be feeling stress with his wife just dead? We got to the house and someone answered the door. I was never alone with an older brother again.

THREE-YEAR-OLD ANTONIO didn't want to be alone in the bathroom. He insisted that I stand at the door while he was on the toilet. I was not sure if he was afraid of falling in or getting sucked down the drain. I left the door open a crack.

"Are you almost done, Antonio?"

"My penis look like an apple . . . now . . . it's a . . . peach!"

What in the world is he doing?

"It's a elephant!"

Oh, my God. "Antonio, you need to finish up now."

"Look how big it is—me show Cissy!"

Still outside the door, I said, "No, no, no, you don't show Crystel. That's your privates. I'm shutting the bathroom door. When you're done, come to the living room and we'll read a book. And . . . and . . . wash your hands when you're done. "

The words worked and Antonio did as he was told.

I asked Jody once, "Are you ever afraid of me touching Antonio or Crystel?" I was almost crying. What if she said yes, she was afraid. What then?

"It never occurs to me," she said. "I trust you."

IN MY EARLY TWENTIES, I asked my mother to come to a therapy session.

"Did the incest start with me?" I asked. I had to know.

"I don't know how the boys learned what they did," my mother said. Then she laughed. "I touched their penises in the crib. It was cute the way they'd stick up."

Barely breathing in my chair, I held the pillow to my stomach and kept it between me and my mother. I hoped the therapist was taking notes.

According to statistics, I should be a pedophile. Forty to eighty percent of pedophiles were raped as children. Pedophiles often target and abuse children who were the same age the predator was when she or he was first sexually abused. It took me many, many, diapers before I believed that I was not my mother.

In my early twenties, I cautiously watched myself around my nieces and nephews, probing every thought I had, every move I made. I feared becoming what I most hated. At twenty-two, Tina, my oldest niece, had rotary cuff surgery and stayed with me to recuperate. She needed help putting her bra on and taking it off. I wasn't any help. I wouldn't touch her breasts and place them into the cups.

"I'm rollerblading in a marathon with my nephew, Steve," I told my energy worker that summer. "It will be just him and me for the weekend in Duluth. I'm nervous. He's thirteen years old and we haven't spent any time together by ourselves. We'll be together for two nights."

"What are you worried about?" she asked.

"I don't want to be inappropriate with him. Stare at his body or anything. You know I always saw my brothers naked. I watched them change from babies to boys, to pre-teens, to adolescents, to men. I have all this information that I shouldn't have. I never had to be curious."

"What do you think you'll do?"

"Nothing. I just keep thinking about my mom, wondering if I'm like her."

"Go and have a good time. I'm not concerned."

When my nephew, Dan, was on break from college, he lived with me and Jody for two summers. I never saw him naked, or him me. I always asked or forewarned him when I needed to go into his living space.

How easy it was to give each other privacy.

ANTONIO CAME OUT of the bathroom. I reached for *Love You Forever* by Robert Munsch on the bookshelf.

"Cissy read, too?"

"We could ask. She's playing with her dollhouse."

He ran to her room.

Antonio returned holding Crystel's hand. Both of them jumped up on the couch beside me and rested their heads against my body.

"A mother held her new baby and very slowly rocked him back and forth, back and forth, back and forth. And while she held him, she sang, 'I'll love you forever, I'll like you for always, as long as I'm living, my baby you'll be.'"

Antonio and Crystel snuggled even closer when we reached that same spot we always did, where my chest filled up and the tears started. "The son went to his mother. He picked her up and rocked her back and forth, back and forth, and he sang her this song: 'I'll love you forever, I'll like you for always, as long as I'm living my Mommy you'll be.'"

"Let me see," Crystel said. "Let me see."

Crystel lifted up my glasses and touched my tears. "Read it again, Mommy, read it again."

THAT EVENING WHEN JODY was helping Antonio with his bath, he said with pride, "I touch my penis in my bedroom."

She caught her breath. "That's good, Antonio. That's where you're supposed to touch your privates."

He fumbled with a yellow ducky toy. "Cissy have penis?"

Jody pulled back slightly, holding the washcloth. "No, Crystel has a vagina."

His eyes widened. "Her vaginuts get big like my penis?"

"No, no, vaginas are different," she said. She stood and reached for a bath towel. "Time to dry you off, big boy."

BEING THE STAY-AT-HOME MOM, I learned to listen for silence.

During the day, I began to perceive disquiet in the air, the sudden shutting of doors, lights out, and whispers. The closed doors really got to me. What was going on? I didn't want Antonio and Crystel to freak out and think that I thought that they were showing and telling, playing doctor, or putting anything they could find into every orifice of their bodies, yet that was exactly what I thought they were doing. I was afraid to open their door.

What was my past and what was the present?

I didn't know what to do. I called and made an appointment with my energy worker. Then I called Jody at work. "What should I do? Should I knock before opening their door?"

She was silent for a moment. "Tell them no doors closed, that you want to hear if someone needs help."

I listened for tension in the air. When the air churned, like frenzied fish feeding, it was then a door would close. I lived in this constant state of frenetic energy growing up.

In the coming weeks, during bath time and getting dressed, Jody and I talked with the children about their privates and what private meant. I reminded myself that Antonio was a toddler. He was not my brothers.

The energy worker assured me that what I was going through was normal and she trusted that I would know what to do when anything came up.

ANTONIO, CRYSTEL, AND I attended Early Childhood Family Education. One morning at a parents' session, I asked, "What is normal sexual development for children?" The facilitator and seven other parents of two– and three-year-olds didn't respond. It was clear that I asked something unexpected, maybe even inappropriate.

Over stale coffee and old chocolate-chip cookies, the discussion moved to bossy three-year olds and what to do if they wouldn't share their toys. I frowned. Sighed. Fidgeted until it was time to gather up Antonio and Crystel.

That afternoon, I Googled sexual development. I went to the library and checked out books from the library: *Everything*

You Never Wanted Your Kids To Know About Sex, But Were Afraid They'd Asked: The 26 Secrets To Surviving Your Child's Sexual Development From Birth To Teens; Sex Is Not A Four-Letter Word: Talking Sex With Your Children Made Easier; From Boys To Men; Parents' Answer Book; and *Common Sense Parenting.*

I learned that beginning in the womb, every ninety minutes boys experienced an erection and girls experienced vaginal lubrication. This normal sexual phenomenon continued until toilet training. From then on, this was continued by all of us only during sleep. I learned that boys might point their penis at a parent like a gun, and not to let it bother me. I learned that children might masturbate more between the ages of two and five than later in childhood. I learned that if I found my children playing "I'll show you mine if you show me yours," not to overreact.

At the next Early Childhood Family Education meeting, I insisted that we put sexual development of children on the agenda. "What's normal?" I asked again. Then I asked the other parents, "Are any of your children touching themselves?"

The parents wrung their hands, shifted in their seats.

Finally, one dad spoke up. "My daughter lies on the couch and touches herself. I'm afraid the mailman will see."

"Thank you," I said, giving him steady eye contact. "Thank you."

A MONTH LATER, Antonio asked me, "What's that?" I was in the bathroom brushing my hair.

I looked behind me, "What?"

He pointed. "That."

I turned and looked closely at the shower curtain, "What?"

"That."

Kneeling to his level, I said, "Can you point right at it?"

"That."

He pointed at my breasts. My nipples were pushing at the fabric of my shirt. Heat flushed to my face. "Oh. Those are nipples." Brushing my hair, I casually added, "You have nipples, too. Your nipples will look like Uncle Scott's when you're older. When Crystel is a teenager, she'll have breasts like me and Mama Jody."

I straightened my hair. Statistically, ninety percent of sex offenses occur in the victim's home and are perpetrated by family members, friends, or acquaintances. Even today, an image will cross my mind now and then. I'll remember a word, a scene, a gesture. I'll ask myself, how come I'm not a pedophile? The answer I came to is twenty-five years of therapy.

Jody and I had childproofed the house. But how did you childproof people?

The kids and I were meeting a friend for lunch. She was a woman with large breasts. I really wanted to tell Antonio and Crystel not to stare, talk to, or poke at her breasts. But if I said any of this to the children, they were certain to do it.

At the Chinese Buffet, I was on the edge of my seat watching the children during the entire meal.

ON THE WAY HOME, I remembered how closely I watched my mother in a therapy session.

"Mom," I said, "Both of my pregnancies are from my brothers. I think Thomas is the father of Baby Boy Smith."

At first my mother didn't react.

I went on, "I delivered a month early, yet the baby was full-term. Marty didn't refute that he was the father, but I don't think he was. I think it was Thomas's baby."

My mother's face showed no emotion, but I could tell she was about to speak. "We should have kept him, then," she said. "He would have been ours."

Bile caught in my throat. I crouched lower in my chair, cuddling a pillow.

"He would have been ours. He would have been family."

I wanted verification from the therapist that she heard what I just did.

Mother leapt off her chair, came toward me in an embrace. The therapist jumped up herself, ran over, shielding me.

Sitting back down, my mother said, "Ann, it happened to me, too. My brother Fred touched me when I was growing up. Don't ever tell your father."

"You can't ask your daughter to keep a secret," the therapist said. "Ann, do you understand that? You don't have to promise your mother."

"I understand," I said quietly. "I understand that my mother had only one brother touching her. I had four."

TURNING THE CORNER to our house, a sudden fear gripped me and I pulled the car over to the side of the road.

"What's wrong, Mum-Mum?"

"Nothing, hon." Yet everything was wrong. My fear was that I would not be able to stop the incest. My fear was that Antonio and Crystel would be sexual with each other. My stomach and chest ached. I rested my head on the steering wheel. *But we're not really brother and sister,* I imagined them saying. *We're not biologically related.*

Our house was one block away. "Are your seatbelts still on?"

"Yes."

"Who's your brother, Crystel?"

She laughed, poked Antonio.

"Antonio, who is your sister?"

"Cissy, silly Mama."

I pressed my palms to my eyes, let out a huge breath.

PART
FOUR

PART

FOUR

THE TWO FIVE-YEAR OLDS AND I WERE EATING A LATE breakfast. Light sifted through the window curtain, landing on Crystel. She was wearing a pair of Antonio's jeans, black socks, and a *Bob the Builder* shirt—bright yellow lettering on blue background with a man wearing a yellow hardhat and overalls. Antonio dressed her this morning, I could tell. I overheard them discussing what underwear she should wear: Spider-man, Thomas the Train, or Bob the Builder? "No Spider-man, Toe, too scary." Antonio was wearing a *Bob the Builder* shirt, too, and eating Eggbeaters that I made especially for him. They were exactly the right color of brown and tasted exactly like the Eggbeaters he had yesterday. He took another bite and I beamed a smile.

Crystel broke my reverie. Her spoon was halfway to her mouth. "Whose belly did I come out of?" she asked. "Yours or Mama Joey's?" Milk spilled from her spoon into her cereal bowl.

Her question wasn't totally unexpected. My niece, Tina, had been joining us for weekly play dates. Antonio and Crystel watched as her belly got bigger and bigger, and one afternoon, Tina placed their palms on the spot where her baby was kicking. After she gave birth, we met her baby boy, Andy.

Antonio sat on the edge of his chair. Remains of bitten apple slices were on his plate, but his eggs were eaten. I looked into Crystel's dark brown eyes. "You came out of your birth mom's belly."

"No," Crystel said, clearly irritated. "Did I come from your belly or Mama Joey's?"

"You came from your birth mom's belly." I raised one finger. "This is Mama Jody." I raised another finger. "This is Mama Beth." Then I raised a third. "This is your birth mom in Guatemala. You came out of her belly." I touched each tip of the raised fingers. "Mama Beth, Mama Jody, Birth Mom." I tapped Birth Mom twice. "You came out of her belly."

While she thought about this, I turned my gaze toward the living room and out the bay window to the east. The morning light revealed children's hand prints on the glass.

Crystel dipped into her bowl for another spoonful of Cheerios. Before she brought her spoon up, she paused again. She smiled and licked her lips. "Did Antonio and I come from the same belly?"

I took a breath, marveling at her determination to know truth.

When I was nineteen, I told the psychologist it wasn't that bad. It took years, but there came a point where I just had to ask. How bad was the damage I suffered from sexual abuse? I had learned to live with the abuse as if it were just a normal part of each day. So I didn't really know.

I raised a fourth finger. "Antonio came from his birth mom's belly. He was born in Guatemala, too." If this kept up, I was going to run out of fingers. "Mama Beth, Mama Jody, your birth mom, Antonio's birth mom."

The sun's rays were breaking through the branches of the ornamental crabapple tree in the front yard, landing on our warm yellow wall.

Crystel flopped in her seat. "Nooooo. You make me so mad." She let her spoon drop on the table. Her eyes narrowed. "I'm fustrated." She picked up a slice of apple, nibbled an end, then used her teeth to scrape off the peel. "Did Antonio come from Mama Joey's belly?"

Antonio was sitting on the tip of his chair, waiting.

"No," I said. "He came from his birth mom's belly in Guatemala."

Antonio jumped up. He ran into his bedroom and shut the door.

I let my breath out slowly and reached for his breakfast plate, stacking it on mine. "You're my girl, honey." I kissed her head and gave her a hug. "Finish eating. I'm going to check on Antonio."

Antonio's head was burrowed into the cushion of his blue corduroy glider. I pulled him up, sat him on my lap. He was a lump and, thankfully, didn't offer any resistance. "I'm happy you're my boy, Antonio. Mama Jody, Mama Beth, Crystel, and you are family. "

"No," he said. "I'm from Guatemala." Suddenly, he began heaving great sobs.

"All of your moms love you. Your birth mom, too."

"I miss her," he wailed. Then he softened, rested his body on mine.

I brushed my lips over his bristly hair and squeezed him. "I know you do, honey." I thought for a moment. What if Antonio and his birth mom could meet again?

Often, as an infant, Antonio would wake first from his nap. I would take him out to our swimming pool in the backyard. I'd hold onto his hand as he dove underwater. Over and over he leapt and rolled in the wetness, his face chasing bubbles, trusting that I would never let him go. Coming to the surface, he'd grin through a pane of water then dive again.

"When I first met you, Antonio, you had the widest smile I had ever seen."

"You didn't know me when I was a baby," he bawled.

"That's true. Not when you were a little, little baby. Not like baby Andy. But I had pictures of you right after you came out of your birth mom's belly. You were so new your skin was still flaky on your forehead. When I saw your picture I felt as if we had always been together." I squeezed him tighter. "You're my favorite boy in the whole world. Do you know who else loves you?"

He blubbered. "Who?"

"Your Mama Jody loves you, too."

This started him wailing again. "I miss Mama Joey."

There was no consoling him. He cried and cried. I wrapped my arms around him, put my feet on the gliding ottoman, and we rocked back and forth. This was what grief looked like. His heartbreak touched mine.

I WAS THIRTY, flying across the ocean, when I felt pain so gut-wrenching I wanted to grab my side to keep my innards from bursting. When I couldn't stand the leaking, silent tears anymore, I went into the tiny bathroom and sobbed. I pushed paper towels against my eyes to stem the flow. Crying unstoppable tears was new to me and just as foreign as the Polynesian people I would be spending the next two years with as a Peace Corps volunteer. I was frightened. I thought something was wrong with me, desperately wrong.

I STOPPED ROCKING. Antonio's head lay on my chest, his tears soaking my shirt. What I felt at thirty, he was feeling at five. It took me ten years of therapy, ten years of AA, ten years of hard work to hear, trust, and then follow my intuition. I was leaving the library one day when a bookstand with Peace Corps fliers grabbed my eye. I wanted to do this. I called the Peace Corps office the next day and made an appointment.

How long would Antonio carry his past?

THE FIRST NIGHT IN TONGA, my Peace Corps homestay father sat snug to my body, cloth to cloth, clutching my hand, smiling, proud. I sat on the bare floor, legs crossed, leaning against the wall. I was to live with him and his family for the next five weeks. He didn't speak English and I didn't speak Tongan, but he wanted me to understand that I was his daughter. All I could think about was his hand moving to touch my breasts.

My sense of smell vanished, though lush tropical bushes and ocean air surrounded me. Among the diverse lofty trees were the fragrant pandanus or screw pine, the elegant casuarina, and the mulberry tree, the bark that was used by the natives to make fine-quality tapa cloth. I no longer heard the *tap, tap, tap* of the wooden mallet hitting the bark, placed on a long, wooden log.

But my homestay father's hand wasn't moving to caress my breasts. He was sitting next to me, holding my fingers, my palm, smiling proudly. His smile couldn't get any wider and a gold tooth glistened.

With circuits crossed, I couldn't discern between what was happening in the moment and what happened in the past. Braced against the wall of my own history, my breathing was short and shallow. I took stock of my surroundings, aware that others were seated around us, and deduced that I must be safe. Still, my body was on guard, vigilant.

"Was this a good thing that he wanted to be physically close?" I tentatively asked my Tongan teacher the next day.

"Your homestay father has the highest rank in the village," the teacher told me. "His wife is a relative of the noble. *Faka-Tongan*, it's the Tongan way," he said. "Shame would rain down on him if anything ever happened to you; he is here to protect you, care for you, and tend to your needs."

Tongans were always touching each other, the way grapes bunch, skin to skin, in their closeness. Men held hands, draped their arms over their male friends' shoulders, and intertwined pinkies. Listening to the Tongan teacher speak about the Tongan way eased my mind, but it didn't make my body less mindful, less awake. His words didn't take away the sense of danger.

Walking me to school every morning, my homestay father cupped my hand into his. When it rained, he was a rooster, holding high the umbrella. I walked sheltered under its cloak. I never got used to his display of affection, his way of making me special. I was sheepish, embarrassed, and looked at the ground as we traipsed through the village. I blushed as he sniffed behind my ear in the Tongan custom of saying hello, goodbye, and I love you. His love was genuine—the feeling emanated from his straight body posture, his arm around my shoulder pulling me into his rib cage, and the cheeks that pushed at his eyes when he smiled at me.

FOR THREE DAYS and three nights, my homestay father wasn't home. He was at a kava circle, a funeral ritual, in honor of a fellow Peace Corps' homestay father. Offering to serve the muddy water, I joined him and honored the volunteer and my homestay father.

Stepping into the town hall where he was overseeing the kava circle, I saw I was the only female. Later, I would learn I was also the first *palangia*, or foreigner, to serve kava in the village of Makave, which made my homestay father proud.

Ordinary village life had halted those days and nights. Instead of pounding tapa cloth under the shade of breadfruit trees, relatives were wailing around the deceased body, lying in state inside his *api*, his body swaddled in tapa. Swaying underneath the burning red of the hibiscus and flame trees, villagers were singing Methodist hymns.

Rising and falling, prayers and sermons breezed through the town hall windows, open squares in the mortar. The town hall reminded me of a barn with dirty walls, as if cows, in their hurry to get to their stalls, had brushed the sides. Panes of glass could be fitted to keep the rain out; instead, small gray birds flitted in and out, accompanied by the smell of wood smoke and salt air.

I walked further into the town hall, blinded until my eyes adjusted to the dimness. Men sat in a circle. I stepped to where a man waved. His hand pointed toward a large oval bowl, dark brown in color, wider than it was deep. Tongans shifted, allowing me to sit in front of the bowl. I nodded to my homestay father, who was sitting cross-legged directly across from me. He was the head of the kava circle, because he was the closest relative of the noble.

Kava came from the kava root, a mild narcotic. The kava root was pounded into a fine powder, then mixed with water until the water turned the color of mud. As I sat there, part of the group, I thought about my convictions. Ever since I went into treatment when I was nineteen, I had been sober. It had been eleven years. Was sobriety important to me? No one here knew about my prior life. I could drink alcohol and kava. I could smoke pot.

With my legs bent and to the side, I smoothed out my dress and covered my knees. In this short time, I had become comfortable wearing dresses daily. Seven men were on one side of me, seven men on the other. A Thanksgiving feast, if we were settled around a buffet table instead of squatting on a cement floor. The kava circle felt ancient, patriarchal, and primal.

A sign was given and I began serving kava. I took the kava cup, a half of a coconut shell, out of the large bowl and dished the muddy water into another kava cup, held by a Tongan sitting at my side. This cup was handed down the line to my homestay father, and at the same time the man on the other side held a cup for me to fill before he sent it down his line. Before the cups were passed back to me, any residue on the bottom was tapped out into a bowl that was also used as an ashtray. Refilling the cups, I passed them again to the person next to me, who passed the coconut shells down the line.

The men sitting next to me indicated how full to fill the cups according to the Tongan who would be drinking. When I put too much muddy water in, they dumped some out. Men who didn't get much kava had been at the circle for a long time and were already what we *palangias* would call drunk. I had been told that it took about fifty cups before kava started to have an effect. Some of the effects included numbness of the mouth, a sense of relaxation and, for some people, the onset of hallucinations. This drug also made you very tired.

Should I drink kava? What would happen if I did?

Visiting amongst the men continued after I served my first round of kava. Though they spoke in Tongan, I understood that they were jesting about me. A Tongan asked me if I was married, others started to flirt. I asked if they had *lahi mokopuna*, lots of grandchildren. Nodding and pointing toward the large kava bowl, they urged me to imbibe. It was easier saying no than I thought. I circled my stomach. "*Pookay*," the Tongan word for "It will make me sick."

THE DAY I WAS to leave the island I was frantic, searching for my homestay father. I peered through the crowd of Tongans, searching for his lean form. My eyes finally latched onto him, sitting in the back of the empty bus that would be driving us to the wharf. Then I understood. He wanted to make sure that he had a ride to the pier, so he'd intentionally missed the village farewell celebration to make sure that he would see me off.

I was angry. No one told me this was going to be hard; no one warned me that I'd get close to him. I sat in the front of the bus, away from my homestay father. Tears pushed at me, wanting release. Someone started singing a song in Tongan.

Life was a series of hellos and good-byes. The more you loved, the more it hurt to say goodbye. I didn't join in the singing. I couldn't. It hurt too much.

As the old, windowless bus rumbled down the crushed-coral roads, I focused on fruit and nut trees, banana plantations, the coconut trees that stood tall on the hillside. We descended, against a backdrop of steep, green hill and dense forest, to the Port of Refuge, where aqua and turquoise waters glistened against the darker, inky depth.

At the wharf, dockworkers loaded containers of pineapple and coconut. We received word that we would sail three hours later. *FakaTongan.* It was the Tongan way. I moved toward my homestay father. He placed his arm around my shoulder and I slid mine around his waist. Connected, we walked to the open flatbed truck that would return him to his village. Still holding onto me, my homestay father said, "*Tokanga*: be careful." He didn't finish his sentence because we were both wailing like the native women at the funeral. I hugged him harder. I had a morsel of what a dad could be: Someone who watched over me and took care of me, walked me to school each morning and retrieved me in the afternoon, took me ocean fishing all night long, gave me rides through the village on his large white horse, was proud when I caught an octopus. My homestay father never touched me sexually, which told me more than anything.

Embracing one more time, we kissed each other on the cheek. I walked away, wiping tears that would not stop.

I miss him still.

ANTONIO'S WEEPING ABOUT his birth mom, about our conversation at the table, tired him out and I laid him down for a nap with his music playing. Ever since coming home four years before, Antonio had napped and slept to *Songs for the Inner Child* by Shania Noll. I quietly shut his door and listened.

"How could anyone ever tell you, you were anything less than beautiful? How could anyone ever tell you that you were less than whole? How could anyone fail to notice that your loving is a miracle? How deeply you're connected to my soul?"

Crystel was in her room waiting for me on her tan corduroy glider. She wanted to fill up her humidifier with water.

"No, Crystel. It already has water in it."

She jumped off the rocker, screaming, "I want to do it now!"

We both knew it wasn't about that. She wanted to come out of my belly or Mama Jody's or, at the very least, the same belly as Antonio. Crystel tossed a doll out of her bed then cried for me to pick it up. I did. After handing it to her, she threw it on the floor again.

This time I ignored the doll. "Crystel, would you like me to tell you a story?" She turned away and faced the wall. "It's a story about Mama Beth."

"Maybe," she snuffled into her Dora pillow.

"Mama Beth had a baby boy and I gave him up for adoption because I couldn't take care of him."

She turned her head slightly toward me.

"It wasn't because I didn't love him, honey. It was because I couldn't take care of him. Someone else took care of him, just like I'm taking care of you."

"Toe know?"

"No. We can tell him together after his nap. Later, we'll go to the library and check out adoption books and books about Guatemala. I also have something else you can have." I left her room and came back with a photograph from the mantle above the fireplace. She cradled the photo of me holding her, Jody holding Antonio.

She touched her face in the photo, then she touched Antonio's. She pointed to a woman in the picture. "Who's that?"

"That was the day when your mamas said they would love you forever in front of a judge. That's her. She was the woman who let us adopt you."

"Thanks, Mama Bef." She hugged the photograph against her belly. Then she moved over and kissed me nine times—on the nose, chin, throat, right ear, left ear, right cheek, left cheek, forehead, top of head. And then a hug on each side. This was her ritual. She was very consistent. When I was with others and she was giving me her customary kissing, I let it be what it was, even if it seemed excessive. I used to be embarrassed with her exorbitance, until the words of a therapist came to mind: "Don't ever feel bad about loving or being loved."

"Oh, so many kisses," I said. "Oh, I'm so lucky."

"Mum, Mum, do you have a mum?"

"She's dead." I shrugged.

Crystel laughed, toppled over in her bed.

"I'm glad she's dead. I didn't like growing up so much." I straightened her covers. Kissed her on the cheek. "You and Antonio will have a better life than me."

MOTHER WAS RECLINING with my three younger sisters in her bedroom. She was sprawled length-wise on the bed, one leg draped over the other, a book at her side, her fingers marking the page.

At sixteen years old, I envied my sisters' easiness with our mother as they laid next to her. They were seven, eight, and ten years old. I leaned against her door watching from across the room. By the look in my mother's eyes, I knew what she was thinking: *Why can't you and I be friends?*

I couldn't even tell her when I first got my period.

I was fourteen. My ninth-grade English classmates were itchy with the smell of spring in the air. There was constant shuffling in the room as kids tried to get comfortable in their seats. I sat in the back row and listened half-heartedly to the teacher talk about the book report that was due.

"What's this?" Judy whispered, kicking a wad of paper in the aisle.

I glanced over at what she was pushing aside with her toe and my body began to burn.

Judy cast her eyes around the row of desks. She honed in on me. "It's probably Ann's," she said.

There was laughter.

"Fuck you!" I said, flipping my head back, scowling at her. My brow pinched tight, daring her to say one more word.

Feet kicked the stained toilet paper between desks like they were goal posts. I slid down in my seat, waiting for class to be over.

Finally, one day Mother asked me, "Ann, do you have your period?" She was pouring noodles into boiling water.

I stood next to her mixing a cake, swirling the rubber spatula to get at the sides. Kids came and went. Noise streamed from the television set in the next room. I could hear shooting, horses running. "Yeah."

"What are you using?"

I shrugged my shoulders.

"Jeeeesus Christ! My own daughter can't tell me she's menstruating. I have to ask her. Goddamn it!"

DUST WAS PLAYING in the afternoon light, streaming through the bedroom window. I could smell fresh manure in the fields. My seven-year old sister asked, "How did you meet Dad?"

As my mother started to tell it, I could see the story in my mind. The late-1940s black Plymouth sedan's bumper was dusty. After wiping it off with the blanket that she kept in the backseat, she rested against the warm metal and reached for a Pall Mall cigarette. She spit loose tobacco, lit her cigarette, inhaled deeply. Her bright red lipstick left a mark on the cigarette, which she soon dropped to the gravel and rubbed out. She surveyed the countryside. How beautiful it was here, miles upon miles of different shades of green. Quiet, still, far from her parent's home in St. Paul. Peaceful.

Sun warmed her body. Turning her face to it, she closed her eyes, drawing in the warmth. She listened closely to the birds that sang and caught a scent of the apple orchard. A deep throbbing sound that became higher in pitch, then deepened, reminded her why she was there in Ellsworth. She was there to meet George Smith, a farmer, who served on the same county board that she did. She was a social worker for Catholic Charities. She walked out into the field to meet Dad, wearing cork-soled clogs with two-inch heels. The sweet clover made her giddy. Shielding her eyes with a salute, she greeted him.

Sitting tall on the tractor, he was the king of this domain, this hayfield, and this moment.

"Hey, city girl, did you come this far for a ride on my Farmall?"

Laughing, my mother told us she had thought she should get married soon. Her mother told her she needed to just that morning. "Mary, you're thirty years old. It's time you had children. You're going to be an old maid like your Aunt Dorothy if you aren't careful."

She was always trying to please her mother, but it was never enough. Even a Bachelor of Science from the University of Minnesota and a Masters in social work from Catholic University in Washington, D.C., even serving in the U.S. Navy as a link trainer and assisting in the repatriation of World War II German refugees wasn't enough. Even an audience with Pope Pious XII. Standing in the green fields, her mother's continued disapproval cut her deeply.

But looking at George, she felt elegant. Light was dancing in the grove of trees behind him and she was grounded to the earth. *Maybe we could have a big family. They'd always be fed.* Her father would be happy. He worked the land, too. Her father was a doctor, researcher, and plant breeder at the University of Minnesota, in charge of a potato-hybridizing laboratory. He would have a potato named after him.

"How much do you really know about potatoes, George?" she asked with a smile, climbing onto the back of the tractor.

"I know which end to plant and where the eyes are, city girl."

"That's enough for me."

My mother shifted in her bed. She added, "It was eleven in the morning. We had a meeting to go to. He wanted to stop at a bar for a drink. I should have known."

I walked out of the bedroom, leaving in the air all the unknowns. What if I had a different father? A different family? A different life?

What if I couldn't save my sisters from my brothers' abuse?

MAGGIE, OUR BICHON COCKER, jumped off my stomach at hearing, "Maaaaamaaaa Bef!"

"I'm coming, Antonio," I said. I met him in his doorway, took his outstretched hand.

"Where Cissy?"

"Crystel is still napping, honey. Let's play in the living room," I whispered. "Let's not wake her."

He ran to pick up orange and green balloons that were tied together. He soared around the room, flapping the balloons as if they were butterfly wings. Antonio couldn't decide what a butterfly sounded like, so now he was a bee. "*Bzzzzzz. Bzzzzzzzz. Bzzzzzz.*"

Eventually, one balloon lost most of its air. He asked me to cut it off.

"That's Mommy." I touched the larger balloon. "And this little one is Antonio."

Pointing to the larger balloon, he said, "Mommy." Then he tapped my chest. "Mommy?" Next, he pointed to the little balloon. "Baby." Then he pointed to himself and said loudly, "Me baby, me Antonio."

Now he no longer wanted the balloons separated. He sat on the couch nestling mommy and baby in his arms.

Shortly after Crystel woke, we loaded ourselves in the car. I backed out of the driveway and into the street. I turned left at the corner, then right onto Penn Avenue. Across the street was B'nai Emet Cemetery. Crystel said, "If we die, do we come back? Will I be born in Guatemala again?"

"You get to make up your own mind, Crystel. People believe lots of things. Where do you think dying people go?" I asked.

"They go someplace where there is singing," Antonio piped in.

"I'm going to be buried there," Crystel said, pointing to the cemetery. She paused tapping her index finger to her lip. "No, I'm going to be buried with JoJo in the backyard. I'll lie next to him so I can pet him. I want to be a cat."

Antonio said, "Grandpa's going to die."

My eyes widened. "How do you know that?"

"Because he has white hair."

Jody's dad was seventy-nine-years old. He was in hospice.

After passing the cemetery, I turned left. A man was walking down the street toward us with a puppy on a leash.

"Was I as little as that puppy when I was born?" Crystel asked.

"Smaller. Tiny, tiny, tiny. Remember baby Andy?"

She nodded.

"Maybe sometime you'll get to see a brand-new baby again."

"Can we travel to Guatemala? We could wait for a baby to wake up." (Surprisingly, the children, especially Antonio, had always pronounced "Guatemala" well.)

I imagined us hanging out in a hospital lobby in Guatemala waiting for a baby to be born. After my time in the Peace Corps, I knew Crystel's fantasizing could never be close to the truth about developing countries. I served as an ambulance driver in the Kingdom of Tonga, transporting a Peace Corps volunteer in the bed of my truck seven miles to the only hospital on the island. Tongans had watched the tide suck the volunteer into a blow hole and then spit him out. Pumping on his chest kept him alive until we got to the hospital, only to find out that Peace Corps volunteers would be the ones taking turns using a hand-held respirator for the next twenty-two hours until a Learjet could arrive and fly him to Australia.

Still, I was attracted to the idea of going to Guatemala.

Easy Readers about adoption and Guatemala stuffed our backpacks as we returned from the library. We crowded together on the couch, paging through the picture books. While reading out loud from Linda Walvoord's *Adoption Is Forever*, I started imagining Antonio and Crystel's own storybook. "Before I was adopted I was born in a beautiful country called Guatemala. Can you find it on the map? My home is in Richfield where the star is."

"Mama Bef, let's read this one now," Antonio said. He was waving *Guatemala ABCs: A Book about the People and Places of Guatemala* by Marcie Aboff.

"How about if we find it on the globe first?" I brought the globe down from the bookcase. "Here's Minnesota." I drew my finger down across the flat surface until I hit a bumpy ridge and followed it further south to Guatemala. "Here's where you were born. Guatemala. The bumps are mountains and volcanoes." My heartbeat accelerated.

"I fly all that way?" Crystel asked.

I nodded. I thought about us returning to Guatemala. Jody and I showing the children their birth country. That would explain to them why their birth mother gave them away. "What are you finding in the ABC book, Antonio?" Looking over his shoulder, I read silently, "*A is for Art. Ancient Mayan Artists painted palace walls with murals showing battle scenes and ceremonies.*"

"Did you tell Toe, Mum?" Crystel said. She looked at Antonio, whispering conspiratorially, "Mama Bef had a baby."

"That's true. I had a baby boy, Antonio. I had to give him up for adoption just like your mama gave you up. I couldn't take care of him. When I could take care of a baby boy, I adopted you."

Antonio studied the luggage in a colorful photo of a bus. Suddenly, he shut the book. "Cissy, let's play in my room." He jumped. Ran. She followed. Music floated from his room.

I stacked the library books, headed downstairs to our finished basement, and fished out the lockbox stored under the desk. The house could burn down but we'd find this strongbox and the adoption papers inside. I leafed through the papers for the Chain of Custody document that showed photos of Antonio and Crystel being held by their birth mothers (a requirement by the Guatemalan courts before the babies could be released for final adoption).

Someday they would ask me if I knew what their mothers looked like.

I focused on the mothers' faces. I searched the lines around their eyes. How could they hold their three-month-old babies after not seeing them since birth and not fall to pieces? Then I knew. There was a strong, determined resolve in their dark brown eyes, which were set above high cheekbones. They were going to do right by their babies no matter the emotional hardship.

The birth mothers resembled each other. Both had strong Mayan features, yet they easily could be Midwestern housewives who worked hard and long in the fields, picking stones and milking cows. I imagined the mothers leaving the fields, bathing from a pail of cold water, dressing in their best clothes, taking the bus into Guatemala City, then entering the government office and sitting before a photographer. They watched as a stranger came into the room carrying a baby. Their baby. The infant was placed in their arms. A photo was snapped.

I rubbed my thumb on the edge of the laminated documents. I laminated the official papers, knowing that I would be touching the black-and-white photos, studying the women, and if at all possible, unearthing their sorrow so I could find mine. Abandoning my baby was a grief of such depth that I rarely experienced it. Maybe Antonio and Crystel could meet their birth moms. That was the closest I would ever get to my son. I touched the photo of Rosa, Antonio's mom, and ran my finger down her long black hair. Rosa never told her mother about being pregnant with Antonio. I didn't tell my mother, either, until I was five months along.

My aunt said that my mother was the smartest kid in her well-educated family. She was assigned as a child to sit at the adult table with dinner guests while her older and younger siblings had to sit in the other room. Her job was to entertain the university scholars that their dad, Professor Doctor Krantz, brought home from work. She didn't come from poverty and cornfields like the birth mothers.

Three-month-old Crystel was alert and comfortable in her birth mother's arms. Antonio was squirming, kicking to get away from his mother's grasp. Tears welled up in my eyes. Yes, we needed to go to Guatemala, all of us.

CURIOUS TO WATCH the heifer having her calf, I had stopped my homework. I was sixteen. Usually a cow found a secluded spot away from the herd to calve out. But Dad kept her in the barn. I shuddered, imagining a cow giving birth alone in the field, a ditch, or under a tree. By the time I got to the barn, Dad had the rope tied around the front legs of the calf and was pulling her out. He cleaned out the calf's nose with his fingers. Then, I left.

I sat at the kitchen table, picked up the newspaper, and jotted notes for my social study class. My brother Thomas, the brother who hardly ever spoke, who was in the same grade as me, pushed his chest against my back. He read the newspaper over my shoulder: "On Friday, April 11, 1975 . . . Officials believed the young woman to be in her early twenties though stated she may have been as young as twelve . . . An autopsy indicated the victim was approximately ten weeks pregnant at the time of death."

I felt as if I knew this girl. The girl was scared to be pregnant, so scared that she never, ever thought about it and hoped a catastrophe would happen. She couldn't be pregnant because her world would end if she was. So, she did nothing. I studied her face and even though Thomas was watching me, I touched her dark hair.

Classmates often asked if Thomas and I were twins because we were in the same grade. No, I told them. We weren't even friends, though in classes that we had in common, I slid my test answers over so he could copy. And when we had term papers to write, I wrote two and changed his just enough to make it different. I didn't think Thomas was really my brother. When I got my hair cut, I practiced seeing my brothers and sisters pass before me in the mirror. I could see everyone slide into my face—my ears, my nose, and my blue eyes—but not Thomas, never Thomas. Aunt Kate told me that she thought babies were switched at the hospital when he was born. Maybe it was just wishful thinking, but I hoped that he wasn't my brother, because I became certain he was the father of my baby. When I dreamed about a cow calving in the ditch, I handed my mother a note as she was walking to her bedroom. I hurried back to the kitchen to finish washing supper dishes.

> Dear Mom,
> I'm writing you a letter because
> I'm afraid to talk to you. That's
> why I've waited so long to tell you
> that I think I'm pregnant again. I
> would have told you sooner but I was
> too afraid. I'd like to get another abortion.
> Ann

She stomped back down the narrow hallway to the kitchen and announced to everyone in the house, "Ann's pregnant." Her eyes were hard and cold. "No, you can't get an abortion. You're too far along, besides, your body can be damaged if you have two and you'll never be able to have children."

My left hand was holding a scrub brush and my right a greasy frying pan.

She went on, "I'll never do that again! I'm still not over it!" She reached above me, slammed a cupboard door, and returned to her bedroom.

She never asked who the father was. I finished the dishes and went to bed.

Brothers and sisters quit talking to me except for my youngest brother, Johnny, who was five years old.

I got bigger and bigger.

Still, no one said a word. I was a ghost my family stepped around. If I said anything, they'd jump. Boo, motherfucker.

———————————

"ANN, GET OUT OF THE CAR, you're not going." Vehicles were being loaded for a trip to the Twin Cities. Grandma (my mother's mother) was having a celebration.

My mouth fell open. A brother poked me. I climbed out of the backseat. Shuffled into the empty house. The air was heavy with insecticide. Dead flies were everywhere—on the counter, the kitchen table, the floor. The last thing my mother did before kicking me out of the car was fog the house with the barn sprayer. I held my breath, pulled my shirt up over my nose, and stumbled to open the door to the red-stained deck off of the living room. I leaned over a baluster and coughed.

I sat on the deck steps, positioned my back against the warm siding of the house, and closed my eyes. I heard an echo of my mother's voice from five years earlier when she yelled, "Everybody get in the car! Let's go!" Then she said to Dad, "George, you aren't coming!" I was eleven years old.

It was our annual Fourth of July outing at Grandma's in St. Paul: Langford Park, parade, picnic, foot races, relatives, and fireworks. We kids wiggled, shoved, and packed into the car. For a split second, there was dead silence. Dad's voice cut the air with a knife, "Goddamn it! I'll burn the farm down. There won't be anything left! You'll come home to nothing!" Standing in the yard, overalls on, smelling of farm and whiskey, he glared at us. Mother was embarrassed that Dad was a drinker. She was ashamed of him.

Our barn burned to the ground when I was in third grade, our house a few years later. It was possible the entire farm could be scorched. Our faces turned ashen. I put how dad could do it on the cylinder. Immediately, the cylinder clicked on an answer: Dad could fill up pails of gas from our 500-gallon fuel tank, pour gas around all the outbuildings, make a splashing trail through the house, and end in the hay mow. String a rope for himself on a rafter and right before it became taut, drop a match. That's how I'd do it.

In the five years since, he had sobered up and became a chemical dependency counselor. It was me now who embarrassed Mother. It was me she'd make invisible.

The baby kicked at my ribs. I folded my arms over my stomach.

When the house burned down, Mother told people it was the furnace. Dad said it was Mother. Mother blamed Dad because he was at the bar.

The house fire had happened at nine thirty in the morning. Mother was in the basement doing laundry, folding clothes, while Margaret, Patricia, and Johnny played upstairs. The rest of us were in school.

As soon as Mother smelled smoke, she grabbed the kids, ran to the barn, and called the fire department. The fire engine was there in minutes. Cold and shivering, she and the three kids sat in the fire truck while the firemen battled the blaze. Our big, two-story home collapsed into a pile of burning timber, but they saved the garage.

I imagined what it must have looked like to my brother, sisters, and mother as they watched our house burn, the flames licking the insides of the house. How the fire kept grabbing and grabbing for more clothes, more books, more wood, more anything to keep it alive. How high the flames must have risen in the sky. The neighbors miles away who must have smelled smoke, heard the sirens, and come out of their homes, their barns, and wondered whose house or barn was burning down. Would they have been surprised to know that it was the Smiths'? My stomach dropped, my skin prickled as I thought of the terror my siblings must have felt watching walls collapse in on each other. I could imagine my mother absentmindedly patting her pockets for a cigarette. She'd bum one off of the firemen if she had to.

Everyone kept tallying up what they lost. Change under the bed, a toy, a shirt. Not much, really. But it was a nice house. All those rooms: a bedroom for almost every boy, girls in a huge room together, an attic large enough for a fort, a carpeted family room in the basement with a ping-pong table and room to wrestle, an office with rows and rows of books.

That house made us feel rich. We had it for less than two years before it burnt to the ground and was bulldozed over.

After the fire, we kids were doled out to relatives and friends. My sister Catherine and I stayed at Uncle Floyd and Aunt Myrtle's. The four oldest boys stayed at Aunt Flora's with my mother. The three younger boys stayed at a friend's house in town, and my four youngest siblings were at Aunt Kate's. Dad slept in the barn most of the time, taking care of the cows and drinking.

The fire sucked the life and hope out of all of us.

A fund for contributions was started at the bank. St. Francis School was a holding place for clothes and toys that were donated. Tables and tables of clothes were sorted by size in the gym.

"Ann's wearing my jumper," a classmate once whispered behind me.

I liked the girl, but what if I ended up wearing someone's clothes I didn't like? I pulled at the bottom of the skirt. I had been fond of the soft yellow-and-black fabric. I scratched at the psoriasis on my arm. I felt cold.

The garage was turned into a bunkhouse for the boys. Mother rented a trailer for us girls, her, and Dad.

Catherine and I were the last to come home. I couldn't understand why. I had tried to be good. I had tried to be a mom, even before the house burned down. Why didn't

Mother want me home first? Couldn't I make her life so much easier? When we were allowed home, I worked hard to make her happy to have me: washing dishes, cleaning the trailer, doing laundry, babysitting.

Our next house was a prefab home, three bedrooms on the main floor and three bedrooms in the basement. Catherine, Margaret, and Patricia slept in the same bed in their room; Johnny slept with me in my bed; and there were two brothers to a bedroom in the basement. To me, this new house proved that nothing good ever lasted with the Smith family.

EVERY WEEK, JOHNNY ASKED, "When's the baby coming, Ann? When's the baby coming?" He told me how he shared the news with his kindergarten class during circle time. I patted his straw-blond hair. Noticed the dirt around his ears.

On October 23, 1975, the contractions started after school, around three thirty. My due date wasn't for another month, but the cramping . . . it had to be contractions. Every eight minutes a twisting inside doubled me over.

I sat on my bed, rocking slightly, waiting for Mother to come home from work. My hands trembled. Brothers and sisters were gathered in the living room watching *Little House on the Prairie*. I pressed my elbows against my side.

Mother came through the door, hung her coat in the closet, and went straight to her bedroom.

I waited a moment. Walked to her bedroom.

With a hushed voice, I said, "Mom, I'm having contractions. I've been timing them." I lowered my voice even more. "They're every seven minutes now."

"Well . . . get your things," she simply said.

Mother didn't hurry. She had had twelve children.

The drive to the hospital was thirty minutes. My leg muscles tightened. My breath was short and quick. I started to sweat.

At the hospital, Mother sat next to my bed reading a book. I closed my eyes and listened to her turning a page, a phone ringing down the hall, the murmuring of voices walking past my door. She left the room when the nurse tended to me. The nurse was the same one that I had when I burnt my back a year ago. My face flushed when I realized this.

"How are you doing?" she asked kindly.

Tears stung behind my eyes.

"It will be okay," she said. "I'll take care of you."

In the birthing room, I was asked if I wanted to be sedated.

"Yes," I said in a low voice. I wanted to forget my whole fucking life. The smell of disinfectant was strong.

When I woke, I was back in my hospital bed. I took note of the time. 9:26 p.m. I wouldn't pretend my baby boy didn't exist. I wouldn't make him invisible.

"I was surprised the baby came so quickly," mother said. She rocked back and forth on her feet. Her eyes shone.

The next day I looked at Baby Boy Smith through the nursery window. I knew I was supposed to feel something, looking at the little bundle, six pounds, six ounces. I knew I should be sad. I knew I should cry. Beeps and the sound of humming machines filled my head.

It had already been decided to place the baby for adoption. "The baby won't get a chance in our small town," mother said. "People will always remember where he came from."

My mother would tell the social worker that my baby needed to be adopted through Catholic Charities. I was fine with whatever my mother wanted. Catholicism bound my mother as abuse bound me.

My parents visited, and we walked to the nursery together. We stood, fixing our gaze on the little baby boy huddled in the bassinette at the nursery window. In silence, we walked back to my room. This was their second grandchild. My oldest brother, Simon, had a four-month-old girl, Tina.

The night before I left the hospital, Thomas came into my room. "Ann, would you tell the nurse to show me the baby? I've already been to the nursery and they won't let me see him."

He hadn't said a word to me during my pregnancy. Visiting hours were almost over. The hallways were dim, my television on low. "Did you tell them that you're my brother?"

"Of course I did," he said with irritation. "They still won't let me see him."

I narrowed my eyes. Would he have stopped in my room if they let him see the baby? I set my jaw, pressed my lips flat. "Come on, then," I said. I slipped out from under the thin, white, cottony blanket. We walked slowly side by side, past the nurses station, down the quiet corridor. The fresh smell of bleach was in the air.

"Please bring Baby Boy Smith to the window," I said softly to the charge nurse.

Thomas stared and stared at the baby. He didn't say anything for a long time.

"Well, okay then," he finally said.

Before I was discharged, I made one last visit to the nursery and asked the nurse to point out my baby.

"Baby boy . . . take care of yourself," I whispered.

Mrs. Smook, the social worker, told me I could name the baby, but that his parents might change it. I didn't want to give him something that could be taken away. His mother was already being taken away from him. It would also have made the baby more real to me and much harder to give up. Mrs. Smook also said I could give him a stuffed animal. Stuffed animals never held comfort for me. I asked her if I could write him a letter instead. She said I could. She'd make sure he got the letter when he was eighteen.

I took my time writing and rewriting, making sure that I didn't have any scratch-outs.

> Dear Baby Boy Smith,
>
> I'm giving you up for adoption because I can't take care of you like your new parents can. I'll miss you but I know it's for the best. Your real parents are the ones that are caring for you and helping you grow up. I want you to know that I love you and I'll never forget you. I hope you have a good life. I'll always think of you.
> Love, Your Mom

A few months later, I received a letter from Ms. Smook. She said that the couple chosen to adopt my son were college graduates. They had previously adopted a little girl, who was now three. Baby Boy Smith would complete their family. She had given them my letter. They knew and understood my circumstances. They would give the letter to him someday. The little girl was baptized Catholic and would be raised in that faith, as would my little boy.

MAGGIE'S RAPID-FIRE BARKING told me that Jody was home from work. I was still in the basement studying Antonio's birth mother's photo.

Small feet raced to the back door.

"Mama Joey's home," yelled Crystel.

"Mama Joey's home," yelled Antonio.

I kissed the photo and placed the document back inside the lockbox, letting the heavy lid fall with a thump. I pushed the safe under the desk with my foot.

After the kids were in bed, I stayed up late studying the adoption books from the library. I grabbed a pen and wrote, "Before I was adopted, I was born. I was born in a beautiful country called Guatemala. Can you find it on the map? My home is in Richfield where the star is."

The refrigerator hummed. The bird clock ticked on the kitchen wall. Spirit, the cat, left her hideout in the basement and lay next to me on the couch.

When I told a friend that Jody and I started sleeping apart during the week so Jody could go to bed earlier, she said, "That's the first sign of trouble."

The one lamp that was on emitted weak light. Maggie was upstairs spooning Jody for warmth. Earlier in the evening we had an argument about the dog. Jody told me that she wanted me to take Maggie for a haircut and to have all her hair cut off. Turned out, that was not what she meant at all.

"OKAY, LET'S GET THIS STRAIGHT," I said. "I'm taking the dog into Petsmart to get her hair cut, and I'm going to tell them to cut it short all over."

Jody fiddled with the steering wheel. "Okay."

Halfway out the car door, I paused. The uncertainty in her voice bothered me. "Do you want to take Maggie in?"

"No. You do it."

Hours later, we returned to pick up Maggie. I slid into the car, grappling with a shaven dog. Maggie jumped into Jody's lap, ducking under the steering wheel.

"Let me touch her, let me touch her," Crystel said from the backseat.

Jody looked at Maggie. "I didn't know you were going to have all of her hair cut off."

I gave her a sideways glance. She was afraid to stroke Maggie. Her hands were suspended above the dog, but not touching her. "I told you that's what I was going to do."

"Yeah, but I didn't think that you meant all of it. She's a large rat."

"I asked if you wanted to take her in."

"Next time I will."

In silence, we drove away. Crystel shrieked, "Let me touch her, let me touch her."

———

I CONTINUED TO WRITE: "Many children stay with the woman who gave birth to them. Some children do not. Some children need to be adopted the way my moms adopted me."

I had gotten used to sleeping alone in our bedroom, preferred it, even.

———

I WALKED THE FIRST-GRADERS to their bus stop, which was two blocks from home. It was the last week of September and we were experiencing an unusually warm day. The forecast called for a high of seventy-seven degrees.

"Mom," Crystel said. She pointed to shorn Maggie at the end of her leash.

"It's your turn, Crystel," I said.

She laughed. "You're funny, Mum-Mum."

Antonio noticed Tyler opening his front door. Tyler lived two houses from the bus stop. Antonio took off running. "Save you a spot, Cissy!" He beat Tyler to the bus stop.

Crystel, Maggie, and I were almost there. Antonio and Tyler were jostling. Tyler nudged Antonio's backpack over the curb with his foot.

Tyler was three years older than Antonio and Crystel and attended the intermediate school connected to their dual language school. He was a bulky kid and not very coordinated. When he noticed me, he gave up his spot in line and walked over. He whispered, "Are they adopted? Your skin is white, theirs is brown."

"They were born in Guatemala," I said loud enough for Antonio and Crystel to hear.

Tyler jumped up and down. "I knew it. I knew it." He said to Antonio and Crystel. "I told *you* that *you* were adopted!" He kicked at a clump of grass clippings. "I know why you can't talk to your dad. He lives far, far away and he doesn't have a cell phone."

"Crystel," I said.

"What, Mum?"

"How many moms do you have?" This made her smile. "Three, Mum-Mum." She counted on her fingers. "My birth mom, Mama Bef, and Mama Joey."

Antonio's slumped shoulders straightened.

Tyler walked back and stood in line behind Crystel.

"We're going to Guatemala," Antonio said. "When we're seven years old." He grabbed the strap of his backpack and yanked it out of the street.

"Bus is coming!" Tyler shouted.

"Remember, I'm volunteering at school today," I said. "I'll see you guys later."

On the walk home, I mulled over a story I read in the *Star Tribune* that morning. As soon as the kids were in preschool, I was going to get a management job. But the labor market weakness that began during the second half of 2007 had worsened. The U.S. economy had entered a recession. Life wasn't going as Jody and I had planned.

Since my early twenties, I'd held management positions, first in operations and then human resources. Utilizing tuition reimbursement through companies I worked for, I attained my Bachelor's and Master of Fine Arts degrees.

But now my job prospects weren't good. My creative writing was going well, though. My writing group of six women had become like sisters to me. We met frequently and I could count on them to listen, give honest feedback, and be compassionate. They knew my secrets before Jody did. With their support, I had over sixteen publication credits in a variety of literary magazines.

Instead of turning to the right to go home, I walked the long way through Donaldson park. Maggie wagged her tail. I unleashed her at the entrance, and she sniffed the air. She walked to a row of lilac bushes, a thriving green hedge. The park was empty of other dogs. These days Jody was absent, lost in her work or lost in her biological family. I had given up asking where I was in her priorities. Her father was dying.

Work needed her. We had even stopped kissing goodbye. I continued walking down the path.

Laughter of small children bubbled up at the park. That was our glue, and I knew it. Neither one of us would leave those kids.

Suddenly, I jumped, startled by a biker passing on the left.

Maggie was starting up the grassy hill toward the baseball field. I whistled. "Maggie. Maggie. Come here."

She stopped. I walked toward her.

"Good girl, Maggie. Let's go home."

AT RICHFIELD DUAL LANGUAGE SCHOOL, I walked down a passageway to the gym. The hallway was dim. A group of Antonio's and Crystel's classmates pushed me into the gymnasium. A little girl with glasses, one eye bandaged, yanked on my arm. "Come on, come on," she said. "This way." In the classroom I called her Supergirl and told everyone that she and I had superpowers because we wore glasses. We could see through walls.

"No you caaaann't," they replied. But they wished they wore glasses.

I skimmed the train of heads for Antonio and Crystel. Antonio was at the far end of the gym playing tag with a boy and Crystel was sitting with a circle of girls. I'd ask them later if they were okay with sharing me with their classmates. I paused to kick off my shoes.

"Why you taking off your shoes?" A boy asked. He grabbed for my free hand.

"These are outside shoes."

He answered, "I don't have a mom. My mom's dead."

I eyeballed him. He wore a short-sleeved burgundy polo and black pants, the school uniform. He was the same boy who hung close to Antonio and me when I volunteered for field trips.

"I'm sorry."

Antonio ran up to me. I bent down, gave him a squeeze. Another boy behind us asked, "Does Antonio have a dad?"

Did Antonio and Crystel go through this every day? "Of course he does, silly." I said. "You have to have a mom and a dad to make a baby." I poked Antonio. "He feels real to me."

"I need help." Desiree, an African-American first grader, stood at the door. "I need help in the bathroom." She was sniffling.

Wasn't this a job for a real teacher? Poke me all you want and I was still a volunteer.

Two assistant teachers were sweeping the children into a large circle in the middle of the gym. *What does she need help with? Am I allowed?* I had bathroom accidents in kindergarten and first grade. The nuns shamed me. Even then, I was trying to be a tough kid who didn't go in her pants.

"Here, you guys go ahead." I dropped their hands, brushed them forward. "I need to help Desiree."

"I'll help, too," a little girl said. She wasn't familiar. "See, I have glasses now." She pointed to her face. "I have a lazy eye." Then with pride, she said, "I'm a Supergirl."

I raised my eyebrows and grinned slightly. "Yes, you are." I took a deep breath. "Two Supergirls to the rescue."

Desiree stood in front of the mirror. "My hair won't stay down," she blubbered. "My mom forgot to flatten it before I went to school." Her words came out airy, as most of her bottom teeth were stubs.

I eyed her hair. It stuck up on her head and to the side like fan blades. "Desiree, your hair is beautiful. *Muy bonita.*"

"Yeah, *muy bonita*," said the other Supergirl. She leaned her forearms on the white porcelain sink, tapping her red fingernails to her cheeks, then peered up at Desiree. Burgundy plastic glasses rested on her nose.

"No, it doesn't!" Desiree stomped, swung her arms. Fat tears laid on her puffy cheeks.

I smoothed her hair on one side. It was cotton-ball soft. I was expecting it to be rough and harsh. Jody and I didn't know what to do with Antonio's hair when he first came home from Guatemala. His black hair was coarse, poky, and stuck up. Since we didn't know what to do, we did nothing. It grew and grew like the head of a Chia pet. Finally, I took him to Kid's Hair and told them to use their lowest blade and take it all off, just like I did with the dog. Sometimes I'd point to a Hispanic and ask Antonio if he wanted a high, tight look— his hair close shaven on the sides, slightly longer on the top. No, he said. Having known nothing else, he preferred his buzz cut. He even tolerated when classmates rubbed his head.

When I took my hand off of Desiree's hair it bounced back, only with slightly less volume than before. I was thankful Crystel had straight hair.

Desiree turned on the faucet and wet her hand. She brushed the water on her head. "If I had a comb or a brush, I could do it."

"If I had a brush or comb, I'd give it to you." I didn't know if that was allowed. A long list of rules came home in the children's backpacks. Not sharing brushes was probably listed.

"I need these two barrettes in." She handed me the barrettes without taking her eyes off the mirror and we missed the handoff.

"*Oh*, I can do that." I picked the small white butterfly barrettes off the floor. Holding the front of her hair back, I placed
one barrette in, and then the other. They hung limply.

"Perfect. You look great, Desiree!" I said. "No one else has
hair just like you." That was the truth. From what I could tell,
she was the only African-American in her class. The other
children were Hispanic, biracial, white, or from India.

She shook her head back and forth.

"She's right. You're beautiful," said the Supergirl.

I walked the girls back to the gym. Desiree walked into
the narrow corridor leading to the gym, but would not step
into the light.

Antonio and Crystel were sitting cross-legged next to each
other in the circle. I sat between them. An adult was kneeling
and talking with Desiree near the gym entrance. She started
fussing with Desiree's hair, placing the barrettes further back
on her head. Several children maneuvered their bodies to get
close to me. The circle became unhinged. I scooted backward,
allowing my knees to still touch Antonio and Crystel. Blond-
haired Caleb dropped in front of me, placed himself directly
in front of my body. The kindergarteners were playing a version of duck, duck, goose. I couldn't grasp the Spanish words
they were using. I leaned over to Caleb and whispered, "What
are they saying? How do you know when to run?"

A boy walked methodically behind each person, reaching
to tap a head, a back or shoulder. He had a plan. I could tell by
his deliberate step. As he got closer he said, "*Pato, Pato, Pato.*"

"How do you know when to run?" I asked louder this
time. The boy was getting closer to us. My heart was pounding. "Antonio, Antonio. Crystel, Crystel. How do you know
when to run?"

"*Ganso!*" the boy yelled. He touched another boy's shoulder and off he ran. The boy stumbled, started after him. Around the cock-eyed circle they ran until the first boy slid into the other boy's vacant slot.

The next boy said, "*Pato, Pato, Pato.*"

Caleb bent his head to the side, examining me. "You're so oooooold," he said. "You're like my Grandma."

I smiled. I was fifty and had started receiving AARP mailings. I peeked at Antonio and Crystel. They weren't listening to Caleb and me. Their eyes were following the game.

"*Pato, Pato, Pato. Ganso!*" A boy tapped the back of my head. I staggered upwards.

"Run! Run! Run!" the children yelled.

I ran five steps then fell like a clown. Bracing myself against the floor, I pushed myself up, started running, tripped again.

The children laughed.

I contorted my face as if I was going to cry. The boy was getting away from me. I flailed my arms and legs, getting nowhere. The boy was in my spot in no time.

"*Pato, Pato, Pato,*" I started around the circle. I searched for a girl who might benefit from joining the Supergirl club. "*Pato, Pato, Pato.*" I thought back to the kind man who often visited our farm to buy cattle. I'd run out of the house to meet him. He'd pat my head, call me Beth, and we'd walk hand in hand to the barn.

On the fringe of the circle, a girl appeared frail in her school uniform. Her nose was red, her cheeks flushed, her hair a stringy brown. She didn't wear glasses, but she was Supergirl material.

"*Ganso!*" I said, and tapped her quickly.

She jumped up, and I was in such a rush to run that my legs tangled and I fell again. I was caught in no time and the children laughed. They pointed to the middle of the circle. Our circle was even more askew because children slid to be in the middle close to me. The new Supergirl swiped at her nose and started around the circle that wasn't.

"*Pato, Pato, Pato.*"

From my vantage point, I observed that Desiree was slumped against the wall, never having joined the group. Our Supergirl category would need to be extended to include kinky-textured hair. Then we had that one Indian boy in Antonio's class. Oh, and the boy with no mother in Crystel's. There was the shortest little boy, the biggest little boy, and the one who never wore a school uniform. There was the child that was always in trouble and had to have his own helper. Finally, of course, my own children. I could see now that there was going to be no end to this being different. Everyone would have to be a part of the Superkid club.

On the drive home from school, Antonio asked why he had to learn Spanish.

I looked at him quizzically. "Dude, because you are Guatemalan. People are going to think you know Spanish." I thought of how I wanted him to meet his birth mom. "Your birth mom doesn't know English."

He groaned.

"What's a foster mom?" Crystel asked. "Desiree thinks that you're my foster mom."

The light turned red and I slowed to a stop. "A foster mom takes care of people, too. But you're adopted. Remember that book, *Adoption Is For Always*? The girl found out why her birth mother gave her up and that her adoptive parents are forever. We can read the book together when we get home."

"Just wondering," she said. She rocked back and forth in her seat. "Do you know my birth mom's letters?" She corrected herself. "The letters of my birth mom's name?"

"Yes, I do. I have it in a safe place in one of our files."

She stopped rocking. "You know her letters?" she repeated, lifting her eyebrows.

I looked to the left and right at the railroad tracks. "I'll find it when we get home and write them down for you."

Antonio stared out the window.

"Were my mom and dad mean?" Crystel asked.

This question caused me to pull over, though we were only a few blocks from home. "Oh, no, honey. Your birth mom loved you and couldn't care for you. I had a baby boy, remember? I'm not mean, right? Your birth mom isn't mean, either." I waited until I got a nod from each of them. I needed their birth mom to know that I also gave up a baby.

Once we were home, Antonio and Crystel dumped their backpacks on the front lawn and climbed the crabapple tree. I walked downstairs to the lockbox.

I copied down both their birth moms' names, even though Antonio hadn't asked for his.

Antonio was halfway up the tree. Crystel jumped down from the trunk and came running. I showed her the piece of paper I was holding. "Your mom's name is Mayra. Your middle name is Maya. There is only one letter different. Isn't that something? Your birth mom picked your first name, Crystel, and we picked your middle name without ever knowing that it was going to be just like hers."

Crystel cupped the paper and ran into the house.

"Antonio, that's higher than you were yesterday," I said, shielding my eyes from the sun.

"I know."

He swung from branch to branch. Finally, he was on the lowest branch and dropped to the lawn. He came to sit by me. I showed him his birth mom's name. Rosa. "You know. Like the color pink."

"Pink. I'll remember pink."

After the kids were put to bed, I told Jody that I was going to finish their adoption books. I began sorting photos in the living room.

She looked up from her computer. "I told you that I wanted to be a part of it." She was sitting with her back to the heat register for warmth. Maggie was stretched out next to her on the pet bed. The durable, pillow-like memory foam had a permanent impression of Jody's slender form.

I leaned forward on the couch, making eye contact. "I'm tired of waiting for you. I gave you weeks to give me your thoughts on the stories and choose photos that you wanted in the books." I tightened my face. "You don't realize how important these books are to the children, the questions they get each day, what the other kids say to them."

Jody tucked her short brown hair behind her ears.

"I'm not waiting anymore," I said flatly. "I've already got the story written and have the photos picked out."

Her eyebrows squished together. "I'll take the day off from work tomorrow."

"Whatever." I threw my hands up.

The next day, Jody and I were in the finished basement. Photos were spread out on a table, colored paper was in the printer, and the laminator was heating.

Our elbows bumped, cutting, placing pictures, gluing. We worked in silence.

Each page was laminated. Each page was punched with three holes. Colorful rings held the stories together.

That evening we called Antonio and Crystel into the living room.

"Antonio, sit here," I said and gestured next to me. "Crystel, you sit by Mama Jody. We have something we want to give you."

Antonio wiggled next to me, rested his body on my side. Jody put her arm around Crystel.

I picked up Antonio's laminated story book. The cover read MY ADOPTION STORY. There was a photo of Antonio with a smiling face lying on the corner of our couch. Down below it read, WRITTEN AND ILLUSTRATED BY MAMA BETH AND MAMA JODY.

"Where's mine?" Crystel said.

"Wait. Wait," Jody said. She showed Crystel that her book was tucked under her arm. "Antonio is first this time." After I finished reading Antonio's book, I handed it to him. "Oh, it's exactly what I wanted," he said, hugging the book.

I gave Jody a fixed look.

Jody fumbled with Crystel's book.

"Can I touch the pictures?" Crystel asked with excitement. "I want to pet JoJo."

"Of course," I said. "That's why we laminated every page of your storybook. See what it says? 'I have two cats, Angel and Spirit, and a dog named Maggie. I had a cat named JoJo, but he died and is buried in my backyard. JoJo used to like to sleep in my bed. I miss JoJo.'"

Jody read Crystel's book, her voice crisp.

Both children took their books to bed. When I did my final check, Antonio still had his arms around his book. Crystel had propped a doll up in the corner of her bed and arranged the doll so that the doll was reading her adoption book.

Jody met me in the living room. "I envy your closeness with Antonio and Crystel," she said softly. "I want that."

"The relationship a parent has with a child is up to the parent," I said. "Your relationship with them is up to you."

In the coming months, I noticed Jody having more dates with the children.

BEING A MOTHER to Antonio and Crystel went beyond my wildest dreams. I never thought I'd be a parent. I had a sketchy past with seven years of unlawful behavior, though I was never incarcerated. From seventh to twelfth grades, I stole, beat kids up, broke into buildings, damaged property, shoplifted, forged checks, and lied incessantly. I thought I'd be dead by the time I was twenty-five. And I probably would have been, had I not gone into chemical dependency treatment when I was nineteen.

At the dinner table, Antonio was drawing his depiction of Yveltal, a Y-shaped Pokémon character that was red and black with gray hair in the back. He was using his pencil to shade grayish patterns along the underside of the large avian-like form.

"Is that a mean Pokémon?" I asked.

He paused, holding his pencil in midair. "No, why?"

"Because of those horns." Black horns extended from above its eyes, with a sharply curved portion pointing forward and thinner prongs facing the rear.

He looked at the horns as if understanding the meaning of them for the first time. "No. He's a good Pokémon."

"Both things can be true," I said. "We're not all good and not all bad."

I moved closer to study his drawing. "Antonio, you're an artist. That's exactly like the Pokémon card. You know, when I was in seventh grade, I stole someone's art drawing, put my name on it, and handed it in as my own."

"Oh, Mom."

"What happened then?" Crystel asked, coming into the room.

"I got caught. Had to say I was sorry. It was the Sheriff's kid."

Crystel laughed.

"I have Police Reserves tonight. I'm going to be a decoy for police dogs."

"Can I come?" Crystel asked, jumping up and down.

Glancing at me sharply, Antonio asked, "What's that mean?"

"Noooo," I said to Crystel, then turned to Antonio. "Remember those police dogs at the police station? I'm going to be in a big fat suit and they're going to attack me."

"Oh, geez," he said. He turned back to his drawing, erased a line. "Why are you doing that?"

"It's exciting," I said. I leaned over and gave him a hug. "Mostly it makes me feel good that I'm not the person that I was growing up." I mentally replayed the time I walked into the 3M plant, flashed a stolen badge, and hid inside a large piece of equipment. And then there was the time I stole a police jacket out of a river-town bar. I could so easily be in jail or dead from my recklessness and bad choices. Certainly not here with these two children who I loved so much.

He extended the black horns on Yveltal. "Don't get hurt."

Crystel tugged on my shirt. "I want to go, Mama. I'll sit in a corner and be real quiet. Please."

"Nooooo." I pulled my badge out of my pocket. "Here. You can wear this tonight while I'm gone. I won't need it. I won't be in uniform."

She took the badge, lifted it up and down in her palm. "It's heavy."

"Yes, it is." The silver badge said RICHFIELD POLICE in black writing, and had a depiction of an eagle with spread wings at the top and a circle at the center depicting trees and a man with a plow. "That's my badge number." I pointed to "431."

"Hug, Mama," Crystel said. She wrapped her arms around me. "Meow. Prrrrr," she said, placing her cheek against mine.

"Love you, sweetie. I'll check on you when I come home. You'll be in bed by then." I walked to the door, yelled down the basement steps, "Bye, Jody."

"Okay," a barely audible voice came from the laundry room.

I PARKED IN FRONT of a two-story building that used to be a fitness center. Now it was a dark, empty shell. Police cars from numerous counties were in the lot. I reached for a bottle of water lying in the passenger seat and gave my clothes a going-over—long shirt, long pants, and boots. I gulped the water.

Police dogs were barking. Their ears, like Yveltal's horns, stuck straight up. Through the large front window, police officers milled about talking in twos and threes.

"Hey, here's our decoy."

After introductions, I was handed a brown, corduroy 2XLarge, heavyweight suit. A young-looking police officer helped me step into the pants. I slipped my arms through the padded suspenders. The jacket had hidden front closures, a stand-up collar, and long arms to protect my hands. The back of the jacket was slightly longer than the front to give me extra protection. An older officer, the K-9 trainer, guided me up the staircase to an empty dark room on the second floor. I was a clumsy Michelin man.

"Here's your helmet." He handed me what looked like a padded hockey goalie helmet.

"I'm going to have you lay down in this corner. I'll put a sheet of black plastic over you. The dog has to find you. When he finds you, he'll latch on."

"Do I scream?"

"Yes. Yell. Tell the K-9 officer to get the dog off you once the dog latches on."

I dropped to the floor on my knees, then rolled to my side. I squirmed over to the wall and faced my head to the corner. The officer straightened the plastic.

"Are you okay?"

I muffled a "Yes." It was dark. I was going to get bit someplace on my body. Maybe it would be my arm or my leg. Maybe it would be my back or my shoulder. My breathing was shallow. Minutes passed. There was a movement outside of the room.

A dog barked sharply in the doorway.

"Come out or I'll send my dog in after you. You *will* get bit." There was a short-lived moment of silence. "You *will* get bit. Come out *now*."

The dog entered the room. I could hear his breathing. He stepped closer. My eyes flickered back and forth. There were two or three sharp barks. I sucked in my breath. The dog began moving the plastic around with his paws. I stiffened.

"Get him! Get a piece of him! Get him!"

The dog latched onto my helmet and started pulling me out of the plastic. "He's got my helmet! He's got my helmet!" I screamed louder, frightened. "He's pulling it off! Get your dog off me!" Beads of sweat were on my lip. My hands were clammy.

The K-9 officer put the leash on his dog. "Good boy. Good boy." He walked toward the door. The dog pulled on his leash toward me.

"Are you okay?" The trainer said.

My labored breathing quieted. I nodded.

"The dogs aren't supposed to go for your head. Let's reposition you for the next dog."

I fell to the floor and put my body as tight to the wall as I could.

"Stick your butt out a little. Get your head closer to the wall." He covered me in the dark plastic. It was black again. "Are you ready?"

"I'm good."

There was quiet. I licked my lips. My shoulders tightened. I heard my breath, stared in the dark. *Don't move, Beth.* Minutes passed. I followed the *scratch, scratch, scratch* of the police dog's toenails as he searched for me from room to room. He stopped at the door, then barked.

"Come out or I'll send my dog in after you. You will get bit."

My breathing quieted.

"*You will get bit.* Come out *now.*"

The dog entered the room. I didn't stir.

Suddenly the dog barked, lunged, and chomped his teeth into the top of my head. He unlatched his teeth and bit me again, dragging me out of the tarp.

"Get your dog off of me. Get him off," I hollered. I moved my hands up to hold the helmet on. "He's got my helmet. He's pulling it off!" I gripped the helmet, fingers straining. "Get your dog off me!"

The K-9 officer grabbed for his dog's collar and clipped a leash on him. The German shepherd barked madly and pulled at his leash, straining toward me.

"How are you doing?" the trainer said.

My legs were shaky. I took the helmet off. "Is that blood?" There were droplets on the floor. I touched the top of my head with my fingers. It was tender but my fingers didn't come away bloody. "Oh, that's the dog's saliva on the floor," I said. "I'm okay."

"Good. We'll get the next K-9 ready."

I curled in a fetal position on the floor facing the wall.

"We don't want the dog to pull your helmet off. They're supposed to go for your leg or arm. I'm not sure why they are going for your head." He straightened the tarp. "If this next dog goes for your head, we'll do something else. Are you ready?"

"Yeah." I was sweating. My chest was tight. I closed my eyes, listening. The darkness and my labored breathing took me back to my past. Nobody was all good or all bad. My brothers weren't bad people. Their growing up was as complicated as mine. Incest itself was complicated. I understood how they didn't think that they were harming me. We simply weren't taught boundaries. In its own way, incest made me special. I was wanted for something, needed. At the same time, it was terribly damaging.

As a child and a teenager, there were times my brothers protected me. I was a teenage passenger in the backseat of our car when my two teenage brothers in the front were talking about how they'd beat up anyone who was hurting me. Another time, in a bar, my two oldest brothers were ready to step in, if needed, while I picked a fight with other female patrons.

In the darkness, I thought back to Patrick as a child. A laborer who lived on the homestead committed suicide when Patrick was eleven. We were told he died of a heart attack. I questioned my mother after learning in a local bar that he hung himself in the shed.

"I was worried about Patrick. They were very close," she said.

Could it have been that this man did something to Patrick? Could someone have walked in on this man and Patrick? Could this man have been so worried that he would go to jail that he hung himself? What about a priest? Could he have done something? My brothers often served as altar boys at St. Francis Church. Secrets were easy to breed in any family.

Two sharp barks. My whole body jerked.

"Come on, boy. Find him. Come on." Then louder, "Come out or I'll send my dog in after you. You will get bit." Louder still, "You will get bit. Come out now."

The police dog's breath was loud. He moved the tarp around with his paws. The K-9 officer urged him on. The dog barked, latched onto my helmet ,and started yanking me out of the plastic.

"Get your dog off me! Get your dog off me!" I screamed. "Get 'em off!" I grabbed the bottom of my helmet with my padded hands to keep it on. "He's got my helmet! He's got my helmet!"

The dog was leashed and led out of the room.

"Okay, no more of that," the trainer said. "You can take a break and then we'll have you be a standing decoy. You'll like that a lot better." He helped take off the bite outfit.

A half hour later I suited up again. He was right. I'd much rather have a dog biting my leg or arm. But, still, I was relieved when the assignment was over. I returned home and asked Jody to look at my head. I sat on the couch, pointed to where it was tender. She parted my hair and found marks.

I said goodnight to Antonio. "How was it?" he asked.

"I'll stick with being McGruff at your school carnival."

He laughed. "I finished Yveltal for you Mama. He's on the table. I made him for you."

"Maaaaaaama Bef!"

"I'm coming, Crissy," I said. "Just a moment."

I gave Antonio a kiss. "Sleep tight, bud."

"You too, Mama."

After saying goodnight to Crystel, I picked up the drawing on the table. Yveltal's underside was now bright red, with black markings. Similar markings were on his head and neck. He had a pointed, beak-like snout. Gray encircled his neck and out over his back. But it was his horns that drew me, the good and the bad.

Driving home from the library, B'nai Emet Cemetery was on my right. Our bag was full of more library books and DVDs on adoption, Guatemala, and dying.

"Is there a stone with my name on it?" Crystel asked.

Row upon row of headstones, different shapes and sizes. Some were low to the ground, some towering. "No, Crystel."

"Where are your mom and dad?" said Antonio.

"Dead, dead, dead," I said.

This tickled both of them and they laughed.

"You guys know Mama Jody's dad is dying, right?"

"He's always dying," Antonio said.

I stifled a smile. "Yeah, he's been sick for a long time. Three years. But now he's even closer to dying. That's what being in hospice means."

I turned left toward our house.

After we walked in and the kids were busy playing, I listened to the voicemail. There was a short, teary message from Jody. She was at her mother's house. Her father had just passed away.

Out the window in the waning November light, a chickadee was feeding on the safflower feeder. Others waited in the nearby tree. I called Jody and asked her if she wanted me to tell Antonio and Crystel.

"No, I'll tell them."

I was apprehensive, but it was her decision. If she had allowed me to prep them on how to speak to her, she would have had a better chance at getting what she wanted. I called Crystel to the phone. She laughed manically into the mouth piece. I reached to take the phone away from her, but she tucked the phone to her chest and walked up the stairs. She handed the phone to Antonio as he slid down the stairs on his belly, head first. He stopped himself, held himself up with one hand, and pressed the phone to his ear with the other. I gave him a minute with Jody, then took the phone away.

"Well, that was a good idea," Jody said sarcastically.

"Crystel laughs because you're giving her attention. Antonio's quiet because he doesn't want you to hurt," I said wearily.

WITH JODY'S FATHER DYING, I knew in the coming days she would be even more involved with her biological family. I didn't mind so much. I had the children. They had me.

ON THE DAY of the wake, I waited for Antonio and Crystel to get off of the bus. Antonio stepped off the school bus crying.

"What's wrong, Antonio?"

"Tyler pushed in front of me," he said miserably. "I was supposed to get off first."

"I knew Antonio was going to cry," Crystel said, tossing her hair back.

"Of course," I said. "When your heart or your body hurts, you cry. Mama Jody might cry at the wake or funeral. You might see lots of people crying. And if Mama Jody cries, you put your arm around her, touch her leg, or tell her that you love her."

Crystel stopped walking. "I might cry," she said.

"Yes, you might."

That evening, the children and I got in the car for the half-hour drive to the funeral home. Crystel was wearing a black sparkly dress and Antonio black slacks with a white polo shirt and black tie.

Before getting on the freeway, I pulled into a McDonalds drive thru. Antonio and Crystel split an order of fries and chicken nuggets.

On the ramp leading to the freeway, we waited for the light to turn green.

Crystel asked, "How do they get Grandpa's clothes on?"

I turned south on 35W to Burnsville. "It's like you dressing a doll. But maybe you use two people to slide on the pants."

"Will Grandpa be in a box?" Antonio asked.

"Yes, he'll be in a casket."

"Is Mama Jody coming home with us?"

"No, honey, she has to stay to the end."

"Awwwww," Antonio said. He set his chicken nuggets down. "I'm full."

"Can I have yours?" Crystel said.

Traffic was flowing smoothly and by the time we reached the funeral home, Crystel only had one chicken nugget left.

At the funeral home, Antonio and Crystel ran to Mama Jody and gave her a hug. "Do you want to see Grandpa?" she asked.

Solemnly, they both nodded.

Jody lifted up Crystel, and I picked up Antonio.

We walked toward the casket.

"Stop," Antonio said. We were halfway to the casket. Antonio looked around at all the flowers.

"Should we go to the back room, Antonio?" I asked. "I've brought toys, the DVD player, and movies."

He nodded.

Several times throughout the evening, Crystel took my hand and we inched up toward Grandpa. "You can touch Grandpa," I said. "Poke him if you want." She brushed his shirt first and then touched his skin. I liked that Crystel wanted to "see" her Grandpa. Twenty years ago, I had asked my brothers and sisters if they wanted to "see" Johnny. I was desperate for them to see him. Our brother Johnny was dust that you could sift through your fingers. He died of a heroin overdose when he was twenty-nine. My dead mother's words came back to me: "There's a spot for the first four of you that die. You can put six urns right next to each other. Me and Dad right here, and then four more." My parents had been dead for six years.

I TOOK THE SMALL CARDBOARD box that contained Johnny's remains and placed it on the church pew. Then I called my nieces and nephews over. "Come on, come on and look," I urged.

I wanted everybody to see Johnny. Brothers and sisters. Nieces and nephews. *He didn't make it out of our family alive,* I wanted to tell them. I opened up the twisty on the plastic bag that held his ashes and peered in at the white coral beach.

"That's not all ashes," my fourteen-year old nephew, Steve, exclaimed. "Look at that piece." Steve was Simon's youngest son.

"Yeah, it must be a bit of his bone," I said, holding back my impulse to worm my hand through the fragments to the bottom of the container.

"Jeez, I thought it would be as fine as sand. I can't believe that it's all white like that," he continued.

"Yeah, me either," I said.

"Jesus Christ, Ann, what the hell are you doing!" Simon said, approaching us.

"We're looking at John."

"Oh, for Christ's sake, stop it." He looked over his shoulder at the church entrance. "Come on—close it up."

I stood. "Do you want to see his picture?" I held out two Kodak instamatic photos.

He reeled backwards. "What did you get his picture for?"

I had called the Seattle city morgue and asked the person who answered the phone to take a picture of John and send it to me in Minnesota. "I wanted to see him. Make sure it's him. Do you know how many John Smiths there are in the world?"

"Put him away," he said brusquely.

After the burial, I put Johnny's photos in the dictionary back home. Sometimes he's in the front of the alphabet, sometimes he's in the last. Sometimes he's marking a page if it's a word I think I'll need to look up again. I haven't divided the two pictures. I keep thinking that I need to do something with them, but I never do. Sometimes I look close and say: "Yeah, that's him." His nose and forehead told the story. His face was swollen from the apparatus they put on him trying to bring him back to life. But he was dead and not coming back. I wondered how long he was dead. When he was nine? Twelve? Thirteen? Or did it really happen when he first took the needle and slipped it under his skin, finding a vein? It grossed Jody out when she opened up the dictionary and saw a dead person. I really needed to move the pictures someplace, but I wasn't sure where. I wanted to always be able to find him.

AT THE CLOSE of the wake, the children said goodbye to Mama Jody. "We'll see you at home." I gave her a hug. Hustled the children in the car.

"Can I have this chicken nugget?" Crystel said.

"It will be cold," Antonio said. "Ice cold."

Crystel took it. "Feels just like Grandpa. I'm going to eat Grandpa." She made chomping noises eating the nugget.

I didn't share this story with Jody. It would just make her mad. These days I was careful with what I told her.

MONTHS LATER, TRAVELING the length of Guatemala, stopping in the seven-year-olds' birth villages became a safe way to answer the question, "Whose belly did I come out of?" Every Guatemalan woman could be Antonio or Crystel's mother, grandmother, or aunt. Every child could be a sister or brother.

"Are you going to Guatemala?" asked the airport ticketing agent. Her red scarf was tucked inside her blue pinstriped blouse. She had prim, short hair.

"Yes, we are," I said. My eyes met Jody's. Was she remembering, like I was, our first trip to Guatemala? I handed over our passports.

She set the passports on her right and the airline tickets on her left. She matched one passport to one airline ticket. She looked up. Her eyebrows were furrowed. Her gaze swept over all of us. She looked back down. Her face tightened and she spoke low to the ticketing officer standing next to her.

I shifted my weight from one leg to another. Deep in my bag if we needed them were copies of the children's Certificate of Citizenship papers, birth certificates, and the Adoption Decrees. I even packed family photos.

The ticketing agent matched the second passport to an airline ticket.

Antonio was tired, leaning on the handle of his carry-on.

Recently, I had read an account of a person not being able to board a flight because the color of their skin was not the same as their child's and they didn't have proof to state otherwise.

The agent's voice startled me. I turned back to her. "You have a nice family," she said. Her voice was sincere. "Enjoy your flight."

"Thank you." I clasped my hands to my chest. She recognized we were a family.

Waiting to board, I handed Jody the itinerary. We would be traveling north as far as Tikel and south as far as Amatitlan. To plan for our trip, I had read blogs written by Peace Corps volunteers living in Guatemala as well as the usual travel guides: *Frommer's*, *Moon*, *Fodor's*, and *Lonely Planet*. I had adoption documents translated and though we wouldn't be visiting the birth moms, we'd travel to their village, shop in their local market, and walk their dusty streets. Our eyes would gaze upon the same mountains and volcanoes that theirs did.

On the plane, Christians saving Guatemalans were seated around Jody and me. Their main goal in Guatemala would be to assist with construction in a village and teach Bible school. Antonio, Crystel, and Jody were seated together in one row and I was seated one row behind them. The missionaries were friendly with both Jody and I until they inferred that we were a couple, at which point they faced the front and quit speaking to us. Their disdain was palpable.

"Mama, a mama bunny," Crystel said. The seven-year-old was on her knees, looking over her seat at me. She pointed out the window at a bunny cloud. The night before we had read *The Runaway Bunny* by Margaret Wise.

"If you run away from me, I will run after you, for you are my little bunny," I said to Crystel, wrinkling my nose.

She laughed, her brown eyes twinkling. She turned back in her seat.

I gazed upon the bunny cloud, loving my daughter. Fire radiated from my chest. The stewardess came down the aisle offering alcohol, soda, water, and coffee. Jody and I each had over thirty-four years of sobriety. "Coffee, thank you."

During our ten-day trip, Jody and I had agreed to tell others that we were sisters. We didn't wear our matching rings or necklaces. Most Guatemalans were members of the Catholic, Fundamentalist Protestant, or Eastern Orthodox churches, which all believed homosexuality was immoral. Five years earlier, at least thirteen transgender women and gay men were murdered in Guatemala. Crimes on the basis of sexual or gender identity were tolerated by the government.

The mission group's scorn toward Jody and me reminded me that it was still illegal for homosexuals in Guatemala to adopt children. Our first priority on our trip was to keep Antonio and Crystel safe.

After landing in La Aurora International Airport in Guatemala City, Crystel said, "We're in my world now."

She was right about that. Less than three weeks earlier, the Pacaya volcano erupted, followed by several tremors. Three inches of ash rained down. Two days after Pacaya blew, Tropical Storm Agatha slammed the country, making it difficult to remove the ash. Heavy rains washed away bridges, filled villages with mud, and triggered a giant sinkhole. Thick black ash still coated the runway. The gritty black sand was being swept into piles. Looking at the ash, I wondered if Antonio and Crystel's birth families could imagine their seven-year-old with them. My son was ten when I could imagine a life with him. It would have been just over six years since their birth moms held them in their laps. Circumstances could have changed their lives, just like mine had changed.

Inside the airport, Crystel walked to a poster hanging on a wall. An indigenous Mayan woman was gazing at a volcano. Her back was to us and the colorful sling that she was wearing held a baby. Crystel posed in front of the poster. I snapped a photo. We now had a complete picture of an indigenous Mayan woman.

I WAS THE FIRST to wake the next morning in Flores. I slipped out to our balcony. I was immediately immersed in a jungle setting. Toucans, macaws, parakeets, flycatchers, warblers, and other birds filled the air. I sat, stunned by the scenery. We had arrived in the dark and had gone directly to bed. Birds of all colors flitted through the air. Allspice, maya nut, and chicle trees (for making chewing gum) were everywhere, along with the enormous Ceiba, the national tree of Guatemala. I stood, leaned over the balcony. To the left of me was a lagoon. Crocodiles came to the surface.

DURING THE FIRST PART of our trip, we took a horseback ride through the foothills of the Maya Mountains. In single file, each on our own horses, we followed the guide into the jungle forest. Liana vine, a long-stemmed woody vine, was rooted in the soil at ground level and used the tree for vertical support to climb to the canopy to get access to the sun. Every tree had a patch of moss, fungi, and orchids growing from it. A loud, eerie roaring reached us. I got chills. The guide told us it was howler monkeys.

Even though it was about eighty degrees, all of us were wearing long pants to make sure our legs didn't get chafed by the horses and long sleeves for the insects. The humid warmth was a hug.

Antonio rode his horse like a pro, keeping his back straight and the balls of his feet in the stirrup irons. He gave me a thumbs up. Once in a while one of us laughed nervously when our horses started to trot. Crystel squeezed both legs on her horse, giving him a "giddyap" command with no success. Her seven-year-old legs just weren't strong or long enough to get any response from her horse. Jody was anxious and I tried to stay behind her, although my horse wanted to pick a fight. Her body had contorted into a question mark with her head and shoulders stiffly curving to the right. My horse approached hers with his ears pinned back, snaking his head. He tried to bite her horse's rump. Jody blamed me for this.

One by one, we left the jungle and followed a dirt path into a village. Children walked barefoot in the dirt streets. Homes were dirt-floored shacks that appeared uninhabitable. Discarded materials were used for outside walls and roofs: sheet metal, tin, tarps, palms, slab boards, sticks, cardboard, corn stalks, straw, and paper bags. Hammocks were hung under overhangs or between trees in the dirt yards. Cooking fires were small fires at the edge of shacks. Chickens, pigs, and dogs roamed.

"Hola," I said, sitting upright on my white horse.

"Sssssh," Antonio said.

"Hola," I said again, waving to the children, men, and women sitting and standing who were watching us.

"Ssssh, Mama," Crystel said.

"I'm being friendly," I said. "People live there." I pointed to a shack.

"*We* know that," Antonio said.

To my left an indigenous Mayan woman was hunched over scrubbing her baby in the backyard with water running from a hose. In the front yard, sitting in the dirt ,was a young girl grinding corn with a stone. To my right, a woman stared at us, holding in her hand a shirt that she would place on her tin roof to dry.

Any one of these women could have been their mother.

I DIDN'T TAKE ANY pictures of the village or its inhabitants. In my research I had read that Mayans believed that you were stealing their soul when you took their photograph.

Entering the stable, I slid off my horse. If our trip ended now, I would be satisfied. The village had provided poverty as the answer as to why their birth mothers gave them up for adoption.

LATER THAT AFTERNOON, before starting our hike up a mountain, Jody took a picture of a cow lying in the tall grass, chewing her cud.

"Jody, you heard our driver tell us not to take pictures. Guatemalans will think that we are stealing their land." I jabbed toward Antonio and Crystel. "We have to take care of them."

Antonio and Crystel were edging closer to the cow. Crystel waved grass at the cow's head.

"They will think we are stealing their children." I swiped at the skin on my arm. "Jody we're white." I nodded toward Antonio and Crystel. "They're brown." I shouldn't have had to say any of this. "Give me the camera."

"No." She took a step back, held the camera behind her.

"Well then, just stop it. Put the camera away, for Christ's sake."

DAYS LATER WE DROVE to Rabinal, a small town in the Guatemalan department of Baja Verapaz. The territory was dominated by mountains and we could view the village of Rabinal hours before we reached it. Endless tight curves down the side of the mountain made us nauseated, and we each had taken motion sickness pills. Just outside of Rabinal, I tapped Antonio awake. He was in the front passenger seat. "Bud, this is your birth village." He propped himself up, sat as high as he could, and looked out over the dashboard.

Homes set off from the road were white with grass roofs. Walls were built with mud-and-straw adobe bricks. Tree branches were thick with bromeliads, orchids, and ferns. Schoolchildren, dressed in white shirts and blue shorts, played soccer in the dirt schoolyard. Were any of them his siblings? On the side of the road was a barefoot boy Antonio's age carrying a load of sticks bundled on his back. Next to him walking was a young girl wearing a colorful print shirt with a basket of produce on her head.

Our driver, Carlos, smiled at Antonio. "Antonio, you come from a nice village."

Antonio straightened even more and gave Carlos a knowing grin.

Carlos was a tall, lean Guatemalan man with a gentle way about him. He enjoyed showing the children their birth country. Jody and I hadn't hid our relationship from him or that both of us were mothers to Antonio and Crystel.

Facing Rabinal's village square was a grand, colonial-era Catholic church. A woman, dressed in bright colors, was standing in the bed of a pickup and preaching the Bible through a megaphone. She had a wide face and a long braid flowing down her back. Her voice was carried through the market, mixing with Achi Mayan dialects and Spanish.

"Let's go to the market first. Antonio, you can pick something from your village to bring home."

The scent of herbs, roasted corn, and burning wood was in the air.

At the entrance to the market was a stand selling *chuchitos*: shredded meat and vegetables stuffed in ground corn and mounds of dried chiles. Next to it was a stand selling juice in baggies with a straw sticking out of the plastic. A step away, rice and beans simmered atop a wood-burning fire.

We followed a Mayan woman with a baby strapped on her back into the market. Stand after stand was filled with fruits and vegetables, woven baskets, cotton fabrics, ceramics, wood products, ceremonial and party masks, candles, leather goods, rope, and fireworks. Antonio chose a multicolored hammock made out of netting.

Carlos helped negotiate the cost of the hammock.

The vendor, a native woman, scrounged around the front of her blouse and pulled out a wad of folded bills. Her colorful skirt was pieces of woven cloth wrapped around her body.

"Mom, you're staring," Antonio said.

"Antonio, just think, this is where your people are from."

Rosa, Antonio's birth mother, was a domestic in Guatemala City, returning monthly to visit her mother and young daughter. Maybe she was here. Maybe his grandmother was here. An old lady was waving flies off tomatoes. Maybe it was her.

"Antonio, I want you to be proud of where you come from." I spun around. There was bustling in every corner, from a woman making purple corn tortillas to women selling piles of potatoes, mangoes, and peppers. A woman in *traje* (traditional dress) was squatting, sorting through strawberries and placing them carefully in groups on a blanket for selling. Pigs squealed. I thought back to being raised on a farm. "When people ask me about my past, what do I say?" I once asked a therapist. I was worried about explaining years of abuse and therapy.

"Tell them it's complicated," she said.

On a wooden table, second-hand clothes purchased in bulk from the U.S. were being resold. The woman behind the table was wearing a heavy red-and-white skirt and multicolored blouse. She smiled. She had no teeth. "Hola," I said.

Crystel was watching a girl her age who had a miniature backstrap loom tied to her waist. She was weaving friendship bracelets. Her blouse was heavily brocaded in blues and greens.

"Let's go, Mom." Antonio took my arm.

Outside the church we bought two short white candles for Antonio. Inside were low tables of burning candles placed throughout the church. The high ceiling was blackened by years of burning incense. Antonio lit a candle for Rosa and then one for his grandfather who was killed in the Rabinal massacre in 1981.

The Guatemalan woman who was witnessing for Jesus stopped Jody and I as we were coming out of the church. She was frantically waving her hands in front of us speaking fervently.

"Carlos, what does she want?" I asked.

He stepped in, calmed her with a low tone. "Nada," he said. "I told her you were sisters."

"Sisters," Antonio said loudly. He shook his head back and forth. "They're not sisters."

CRYSTEL'S VILLAGE WAS a few hours from Rabinal, just south of Guatemala City. In front of us, a colorfully painted old school bus was staffed by a driver and a man who hung off the side of the bus, yelling "*Ciudad Vieja! Ciudad Vieja!*" The bus stopped when an old woman with a basket on her head and a woman with a baby wrapped on her back wanted to get on. Children's heads bobbed out the windows and people stood in the aisle. The chicken bus coughed black smoke and weaved up and down the mountain, cutting corners and sharp bends. The jungle was beneath and above us. On the road into Guatemala City, pickups carried large blue containers. They were full of milk, Carlos told us. Cattle, pigs, and people in the back of pickups were also being transported into the city.

Arriving at San Miguel Petapa, there were slices of stores, like slices of bread in a loaf. Population: 94,228. Uniformed guards with short assault rifles stood at every slice. Was I wrong that this was Crystel's birth village? I pulled the paper from my pocket. San Miquel Petapa was penciled on the thin white sheet.

"Carlos, should we stop or keep going?"

"Keep going."

"Crystel, this is your village, but we'll go to Amatitlan, where you were born in the hospital. It's only twenty minutes away," I said.

The town of Amatitlan was situated at the head of the Michatoya River, which was the outflow for Lake Amatitlan. The lake was quiet and there were many market stands to

choose from for lunch. Crystel bypassed many handicraft
stalls to buy a floppy pink polyester sun hat to bring home.
One that we could easily get at a dollar store in Richfield.

Jody and I shrugged.

"Mama, we go to the volcano now?" Crystel said.

"Yes, honey." Lake Amatitlan was situated in a large
caldera at the northern base of Pacaya Volcano. One of
Crystel's classmates told her that her birth mother was probably killed when the volcano erupted. She came home from
school in tears, worried that her birth mom was dead.

It had been twenty-seven days since the eruption.

About 9,000 people lived within three miles of the active
cone. Hundreds of evacuated villagers had started to return
to their homes.

Initially, the road to the volcano was paved. We climbed
up and up the steep, windy road. Fields of coffee plants were
dusted with volcano ash. Occasionally, we drove past indigenous women wearing colorful floral dresses, balancing items
on their heads, going up and down the mountain.

"See, Crystel," I said. "Your birth mom's all right."

I didn't know this. Her birth mom didn't live on the volcano. She lived 4.9 miles away in San Miguel Petapa, where
the soldiers stood armed with assault rifles at every storefront.
I had read that roofs collapsed on houses in San Miguel Petapa
due to the accumulation of ash, sand, and volcanic stones.
Residents were still re-roofing and shoveling out homes.

The road to Pacaya Volcano had changed from paved to
unpaved, and was deeply rutted. The road was covered in fine
dust and stones. Three Guatemalan children of Antonio's and
Crystel's age were hauling scavenged firewood tied to their
backs toward a home where the walls were made of cornstalks

and the roof thatched. Carlos drove around fallen rocks. He slowed the four-wheel drive vehicle to a crawl amid huge clouds of dust.

Driving through several villages, we saw stray dogs sleeping or wandering. Roosters crowed. Clothing was laid out to dry on tin roofs or strung over fences. A man wearing striped pants and a Panama hat leaned against a dusty, concrete corner building and watched us drive slowly by. *Don't doubt the human spirit,* he seemed to be saying with his fine dress. His head was cocked to the side, his arms crossed. Humans would rise even amid ruin.

Coming around a curve, we met a group of men walking down the mountain carrying a small white casket above their heads. A flow of men, women, and children followed.

Carlos pulled over at the sign: BIENVENIDOS SENDERO CERRO RIOS DE LAVA.

"What does it say, Carlos?"

"Closed. Lava rivers."

He pointed to the smoking volcano and the bright orange lava flow. The air smelled like burnt toast. Carlos's white car was unrecognizable with the layers of dust coating the paint. We walked past the sign and picked up tephra, rock fragments and particles ejected by the volcano. A Guatemalan boy with worn jeans and a tattered black t-shirt sat on a boulder. Carlos nodded toward him. I took a few Quetzals from my pocket and placed them in the boy's open palm. I had a lump in my throat. He could have been Antonio or Crystel.

FOUR CARRY-ONS WERE on our back porch in Minnesota. Clothes that needed washing were in a pile. Handicrafts were spread out on the floor. Antonio picked up a small blue-and-white Guatemalan flag. I identified the Resplendent Quetzal in the center of the flag.

Crystel was handling a small baggie of black volcanic porous rock that she took out of her suitcase. She opened the bag, took out a rock. She fingered the small rock, studied the spaces and holes. "I want us to find my birth mom."

I straightened up from my suitcase. This didn't surprise me. Crystel was always ready for her next step, just like I was.

Jody was waiting for me to respond. The veins were tight on her neck.

"Crystel," I said.

"Yes, Mama."

"You remember the story of the runaway bunny?"

"The one where the mommy bunny goes after the little bunny no matter where he goes?"

"Yes, that one." I swallowed hard. "I'll be the mama bunny. And wherever your birth mom is, we will find her."

When I said these words I knew that was exactly what I had to do, what I was called to do. Telling these women that I, too, had given up a son, would be righting something in the Universe.

PART
FIVE

I LOOKED FOR MY SON EVERYWHERE: IN CONVERSATION WITH others who had adopted children, in children the same age as my son, in young adults who told me they were adopted. I didn't request my son's formal adoption records. I didn't feel as if I had the right. I gave him up. He was someone else's son. But more than that, what stopped me was this: what would I tell him about his father? I researched babies born as a result of incestuous unions. Statistics showed that only a small percentage of such children had difficulty. In my early twenties, I wrote a letter to Mrs. Smook telling her that my brother could be my son's father. Maybe he was having trouble and this information would be helpful. My son was my son, and I loved him. If he wanted to find me, he could. I registered on the Soundex Reunion Registry.

Three years before adopting Antonio and Crystel, in a graduate writing course, I studied a lean young man with brown hair who sat across from me. Each class, I picked up bits of his adoption story from a narrative he was crafting. While he shaped his memoir, I stitched together a poem.

Reflection

I want to know if you wonder if she's your mother
when you hear a bit of her story
and she gets to the part where she's given
up a son at birth.

I want to know if you have a checklist
to cancel out the possibility.

I listened for any mention of a sister who was three years
older than him.

And if you do, I want to know if you start with skin tone
then move to the tint and texture of her hair,
the color of her eyes, the shape of her face,
the length of her fingers.

I listened for his birthdate.

Or, do you go right to her age,
where she was raised,
and the time of year
she gave birth?

I listened for where he was raised.

Or, is it her personality and mannerisms
which intrigue you? Is she talkative
or shy and lives inside?
Does she move to touch her brow
and is her voice gravelly?

I listened for his parents' occupations.

> I do the same
> starting with the question
> are you my son?

At the end of the semester I gave Steven, the graduate student, this poem. I wanted him to understand that a birth mother never forgets her baby.

Steven thanked me through an email.

> I've just recently began the "search" process and I was appalled at the politics and money involved in something as sacred as a son's curiosity about his mother. I've grown so angry at the system that I have never even considered what a toll adoption must take on the birth mother, and what questions she asked herself.
>
> Finally, I was able to give my mythical birth mother some reality because I've met, been given a poem by, someone who's lived the other end of the story. I expect that it will inspire me to look at my writing differently and explore this notion that she could be anywhere, and she could be asking the same questions of me that I've been asking of her all these years. I couldn't imagine living a whole life—a life she gave me—without meeting her, and so I must try, no matter what the financial and emotional costs.
>
> I expect no explanation, no commentary of any sort. If we only met briefly once, it will be enough.

AFTER RECEIVING STEVEN'S email, I wrote the ending to my poem:

> Kids like Steven never ask who is God,
> they ask who their birth mom is.

JODY WAS SITTING in her usual spot on the dog bed, her back to the floor register. I leaned forward from my place on the couch. "Jody, have you called your old neighbors yet?" Her neighbors had adopted Guatemalan children several years before we did and had reunited their children with their birth moms.

"No." She kept her eyes on her laptop. Her face flushed.

I frowned. "Just give me the number. I'll take care of it."

"I'm not sure if I can find the number." She cleared her throat.

I stood, threw my hands up. "Jeez. Just give me their names. I'll find the number."

Was she not giving me the phone number because she was afraid of what would happen when the children met their birth moms? Was she afraid that the children would love her less or not enough? Once in a while I felt a twinge of fear, but it was quickly overtaken with a burning desire to make this reunion happen. Steven's email hung on me like burnt skin that needed to be pulled off with a tweezers, allowing new skin cells to form. *If we only met briefly, once, it would be enough.* I would have loved to have known my son growing up. Who he was. How he thought. How he made reason out of life. Most of all, to see for my own eyes that he was loved and cared for and that he didn't hate me.

Certainly, meeting the birth moms would alter our lives. For good or bad, neither Jody nor I could say. The risk was worth it. We could give this gift to our children. To the birth moms. Did I feel more strongly about this than Jody? I didn't want to ask because I didn't want to be stopped. I needed to meet the moms. I needed them to know that I gave up a child. I needed to do this for my son, for all the Stevens out there, and for my own children. Jody had told me before, "Whatever you want, you go for it. That's what I love about you the most." But what about now, when it might be in opposition to what she wanted? What if she wasn't ready for all this?

I jerked the drapes closed in the living room, shutting out the street light. Jody tapped on her computer. She was an excellent employee, always receiving the highest of reviews. She was also an excellent daughter and sister. Though she was the youngest of six, her parents had named her executor of their estate. I watched from the sidelines her efforts to be loved and acknowledged by her siblings. In contrast, I had worked for years to separate from my family. Two years from now, when my sister, Patricia, would tell me that relatives wanted me and my family to join them at an extended family reunion, I'd cry. Patricia would reach out and touch my shoulder. I'd explain through tears that I'd never forgive myself if anything happened to Antonio and Crystel.

"It's not that I don't want to, Patricia, it's that I can't. I love you and all my siblings, but I can't do it. I can't pretend that Antonio and Crystel being abused by their teenage cousins isn't a possibility. God bless our mother's soul, but I won't be like her and not see my children, and put them in harm's way. How can I think that something won't happen to Antonio and Crystel if our brothers and sisters have not ever acknowledged our past? Now they're parents and their kids are teens."

"I understand," Patricia would quietly say. "That's why you and Jody have custody of our children if something happens to me and Roger. I know you won't let them get hurt."

I walked slowly to the couch and closed my laptop. I was struggling with my memoir. One mentor liked the adoption story: *Mama Beth, Mama Jody, A Family Takes Root*. One mentor liked the abuse story: *A Memoir of Incest, Rape, Healing and Hope*. Neither one wanted the two stories together. Yet, I was both stories. The past was my present and the present was a culmination of my past. What was the future of my family?

Downstairs in our finished basement, I laid out my clothes for tomorrow. I was a home health aide now. When I took the job, I was desperate. I had sent out hundreds of résumés for human resource management jobs. Then Tina walked into my house one afternoon and asked me if I wanted a job.

"Yes, I'll take anything," I said. I was at the back door, holding the door open to let the dog out. Tina had been taking care of an eighty-six-year-old woman in a wheelchair for the past couple of years. Bea needed twenty-four-hour care and the family was particular about who cared for her. Her family owned one of the largest privately held companies in the Midwest, where Bea herself had once been vice president. They wanted professionals taking care of their mother. Like Tina, many of her home health aides were studying to be nurses.

I soon became the day aide, accompanying Bea to appointments, theatre, shopping, dining, and synagogue. Tomorrow we would be having lunch at the country club with her family to celebrate her daughter's birthday. I would also be giving my two-week notice.

I added water to the iron. Pressed each pant leg. Flipped the pants and ironed the other side.

Jody came down the steps. "I'm sleeping downstairs tonight with you."

"Why?" I said in a sharp tone, more harsh then I intended. I took the pants off the ironing board, held them by the legs, and snapped them firmly.

"Because we're partners," she said firmly.

I turned away and grimaced. "It will be a while before I come to bed." I removed the shirt from the hanger. Noticed the shadows in the room, flipped on another light. I shook out the shirt, laid the collar flat on the ironing board, and pressed. Next I put both sleeves together on top of the ironing board.

It would be hard to said goodbye to Bea. In the year that we were together, we had grown very close. I turned the shirt to iron the backside.

"Are you coming?" Jody called from the bedroom.

I returned the shirt to the hanger and walked slowly toward her voice. Yes, it would be hard to say goodbye to Bea.

IN THE MORNING, the drive to Bea's home took forever though it was only a few miles away. Every light turned red. I switched radio channels constantly. After parking, I rushed into Bea's home and hurried to her bedroom. She was watching the morning news, waiting for me in her lift-chair recliner. "Hello, sweetie," I said. I bent and kissed her on the lips.

"Hello, honey," she said, kissing me back. "How is your morning?" Her eyes glowed.

My stomach constricted. I pulled a footrest over, sat, and took her hand. I looked down briefly, then into her brown eyes. After a deep breath, I said, "Bea, I got a job as a human resources manager." I sucked in a few short breaths, stuttering. "I only have two more weeks with you." I reached for pink Kleenex on her end table and dabbed my eyes.

Her eyes clouded over, and she squeezed them shut. Tears slipped out. I watched her face carefully for any signs of distress. Lately she had been having numbness in her face, arms, and leg on her left side. We held hands tightly and were quiet for a long time.

———————————

In 1991, I WAS CALLED into the Peace Corps director's office on the island of Tongatapu in the Kingdom of Tonga and was told that my mother had inoperable lung cancer and only a short time to live. My mother had tracked me down. All the information was verified. I was given a leave of thirty days.

Within days, I arrived at the homestead.

Dad was in the yard picking up sticks. Mother and I sat across from each other at the small kitchen table in the fifth-wheel recreational vehicle. Our knees might have touched but I sat straight and alert. She had her hands folded together, fingers intertwined, the thumbs holding each other up. She couldn't seem to catch her breath.

The fifth-wheel camper was their home. Mother explained how she was on a golf course in Texas when she felt as if she was having a heart attack. She went to the doctor that afternoon. After tests revealed her cancer, they drove straight to our homestead on Thurston Hill in Wisconsin.

"I'm sorry about the incest, Ann," she said. She spoke hesitantly, obviously troubled, and twirled her thumbs. She paused, looked to the left out the window. "I was overwhelmed. I didn't know what to do."

I didn't say anything. I didn't tell her that she was forgiven. I didn't tell her that it was all right.

BEA RELEASED MY HAND. "Honey, I need to use the bathroom."

I pulled her wheelchair close to the recliner and locked the wheels. I used the remote control to bring the recliner upright. I positioned myself as close as I could to Bea, then gripped her gait belt. Bea placed one hand on the far armrest.

"Okay, sweetie, one, two, three," I said.

Bea pushed off the recliner.

I pivoted toward the wheelchair. Once Bea's legs were touching the seat of the wheelchair, I bent my knees to lower her into the seat. I hugged her broad shoulders after she was seated, buckled her seatbelt, unlocked her wheels, and pushed her into the bathroom.

After her transfer to the toilet seat, I said, "Okay, Bea, just give a shout when you're done." I stepped back into her bedroom, remaining within earshot.

It was late May. I was leaving Bea the same month I was called home by my mother.

"MY BIGGEST REGRET is having the abortion," Mother went on to say. "It took me a year to get over."

I pulled back in my seat and looked at her inquisitively. It was me on the table, my feet in stirrups. My face turned red. "Is that why you and Dad were fighting about who would take me to the doctor when I burnt my back?" I pressed my right thumb to my small left finger, cracked my knuckle, moved to the next finger, cracked it, too. "Both of you were afraid of what the doctor would think of you?" I cracked my middle finger. "Or, didn't the priest give you absolution?"

Without answering, mother pushed herself up and went into the closet-like bathroom.

What about me? I wanted to shout at her retreating back. *I was only fourteen!*

She emptied her bowels. Then she hacked, her cough scraping her lungs. I stepped outside the suffocating camper. Across the road, corn shoots had emerged from the soil.

I WAS FOURTEEN. The afternoon was dry and hot, the rows of corn long, the cornfield large. My detasseling job amounted to me plucking the tassel from the tender cornstalk, standing tall as a soldier over my head. Detasseling was a form of pollination control, used to cross-breed two varieties of corn. Reaching with my left hand I pulled the stiff insert, yanked, disengaging the bud from its body, letting it slip out of my hand. I moved to the next stalk and with my right hand, stretched, bent the stalk toward me, and jerked the stubborn offshoot. I moved down the column: left, right, left, right, left, right. I paused; let my arms fall to my side and rested, listening to the racket of sixty other kids toddling down their rows.

Left, right, left, right. I started up again. This was the last row of the day, and when we were done we would board the bus for town. I picked faster, not wanting to be the fourteen-year-old kid who needed bailing out.

"MOM, MY STOMACH HURTS," I said, walking into the kitchen, letting the door bang behind me.

"Give it a half hour and see if it goes away."

An hour later, the pain was worse. "Mom, it still hurts."

"Where?"

"Right here," I said, pointing to my side. "It aches all the time and it won't go away."

"All right, get in the car. I'll drop you off at the doctor's and you can call me when it's over."

PUSHING AND PRODDING my stomach, Dr. Klaas kneaded me as if he were making bread. I kept my eyes on the white ceiling while he instructed me to put my feet in the stirrups. Studying the overhead light, I thought about the time I tripped little Jimmy Klaas in church. I was in fifth grade and Jimmy was in third. Did Dr. Klaas know? Did Jimmy come home from school and tell his dad that I tripped him? Did the nuns call the doctor at his office? Had he been examining a girl like me?

"OKAY, HONEY, I'M DONE." Bea stood. I helped her with her clothes, then wheeled her to the vanity. I handed her a glass of water and put a dot of toothpaste on her electric toothbrush.

"Thanks, honey."

I kissed her head and gave her shoulders a little squeeze.

She stood, braced her forearms on the vanity, and brushed her teeth.

IN THE DOCTOR'S OFFICE, I dug my shoulders into the examining table while Dr. Klass pressed down on my lower stomach to manipulate my organs from the outside. He told me to relax and let my knees fall open. I studied how the edge of the ceiling met the wall.

"You can sit up," he said. "The nurse will be in."

I sat, dangling my feet over the side, and smoothed out the wrinkled off-white paper under me.

The nurse opened the door, handed me a cup. "Ann, Dr. Klaas wants to test your urine. Will you fill this up to the line, please?"

Grabbing the back of my gown, I jumped off the table.

A little later, Dr. Klaas returned to the room. "Ann, I want to examine you again."

I laid down and scooted my butt to the end of the table. I focused on the corner of the wall and ceiling. How was a wall supported? What kept it from falling down?

"Ann, you're pregnant."

I waited in silence.

"Is it one of your brothers?"

"Noooooo!" I shrieked, putting my elbows and forearms under me, lifting myself up off the table.

I would come to believe that the doctor asked me if I was pregnant by my brothers because of the high likelihood. At fourteen, I couldn't yet imagine that it was my brothers. What I had learned since was that when people were subjected to a lot of mental or physical pain, they found a way to endure the unendurable—they dissociated from their experience, denied or completely suppressed its memory. In incest survivors and abuse survivors, this meant many of us simply left our bodies behind. Also, I was too afraid of what would happen to me if I told the truth. Mother would rid herself of the problem (me) and not my brothers. That would have been proof she didn't love me. That I was expendable. It was self-preservation that made me say no. I couldn't yet believe that she didn't have what it took to love me and keep me safe. What about my sisters? Who would keep them safe?

"Get dressed. I'll call your mother."

I put my clothes on, hurried out the doctor's office, supported myself against the wall. I desperately wanted a cigarette. Looking toward the hill on my left, I contemplated the fields, the fences to cross to make my way out of town. It had to have been when I skipped out of school and went with that guy drinking by the creek. I had been so worried that no one would want me. Him sleeping with me would mean I was worth something. I contemplated my choices. What would happen if I ran away? I'd still be pregnant. Then what? I'd still be pregnant. Mother's car came around the corner. She parked on the street opposite me. Crouching down on my haunches, I let the building hold me while it swallowed her.

"Get in the car," she said tersely.

On the way home, I kept my eyes locked on the changing landscape. I studied the black-and-white cows, the farmhouses, cornfields, red barns, gravel driveways, ditches, and telephone poles.

"Jeeeesus Christ, I wish it were appendicitis," Mother said.

KIDS SCATTERED WHEN we walked into the house. Mother disappeared to her bedroom with a phone book and Dad.

"Ann, come here," Mother called from her room.

I went into their bedroom.

"Close the door." She sighed. "This is easier when it's not your own kid."

My mother was a social worker for Pierce County. Who was she talking about? Was it a classmate? I looked down. The crevices in the linoleum imprisoned dirt.

"I called Dr. Jonas and he gave us the name of a clinic in the cities." She added, "You're going to get an abortion. We have an appointment tomorrow. Your father is coming. I don't want you to say anything at all to the other kids, to anybody. If they ask, tell them we're going Christmas shopping."

It was August. Why would we be Christmas shopping in August?

I PLACED BEA'S PILLS for the morning in her palm. Filled her glass with water.

"What are you thinking about, honey?" she said. "You know you're just like a daughter to me."

A wave of sadness came over me. I was clumsy and bumped Bea's hand. A white pill fell on the vanity. I placed it back in her palm, stared out the window. A gust of wind came up. White petals fell off a crabapple tree.

ON THE CAR RIDE to the Twin Cities, we sat in heavy air. I got out of the car in a parking lot behind a brick building. In the waiting room, I flipped through a *Reader's Digest*. Dad sat kitty-corner from me, holding a magazine, turning the pages. Was he reading, or just looking at pictures? Mother sat next to him, lost in a book she pulled from her purse. She stopped reading when they called my name.

Five minutes later, I was lying on a table. The glare of the bright room startled me. I could reach and touch the white walls, and if I shut my eyes they'd close in on me. A large light fixture furnished enough heat to keep a brood of baby pheasants warm. Squinting through the brilliance, I regarded the doctor.

He was wearing sunglasses. I tried to peer around his lenses, only turning my head when he inserted what felt like toothpicks.

The nurse explained, "You're too far along for us to do the procedure today. We're placing these wooden tips in your cervix to open it up. They need to be in for twenty-four hours. You'll have to come back tomorrow."

The car was as still as a cemetery on the way home. I sensed my parents' disappointment that this wasn't over.

"HONEY, I'M READY to put makeup on."

I pushed Bea to her vanity table, where she had a silver tabletop mirror with lighting and a full mirror behind the table. Downward-facing lighting pointed at a wall and LED lights were installed to the side of the vanity area. The mirror also reflected light coming in her window.

"Bea, I'm going to run and get my makeup." I had just started putting on makeup in preparation for my human resources position.

"Oh, yes, honey. Do that. Lighting is so important."

Bea pulled a white octagon tray toward her that held cream, concealer, and blush.

I sat my blush, mascara, concealer, and eyeshadow on her vanity top.

"Okay, honey," she said. "Put the concealer on you like this."

"Just a second." I hurried and got a chair from the other room. I sat and copied her. "Like this, Bea?"

"Yes, dear." She looked at me in the mirror. "But you're going to a foundry. Why on earth do you need makeup in a foundry?" She reached for a votive candle filled with makeup brushes. "Aren't foundries dirty, grimy, and full of soot?"

I laughed. "Sweetie, you're right. I took a tour and it was all fire and smoke." I applied light blue eyeshadow on my lid. "Makeup makes me feel better, Bea."

"Honey, it took you long enough to figure that out," she chuckled. "Come here. Let me do your blush. You're lopsided."

She turned in her chair. Our knees bumped, rested on each other.

MOTHER AND DAD DIDN'T reach out to touch me before I was ushered away with a nurse.

I laid on an operating table that was no bigger than a stretcher. I couldn't see what the doctor and nurse were doing, but I could hear them as they bobbed and weaved between my legs. The scraping reminded me of an ear of corn being ripped off its stalk: *keeech, keeeech, keeech.* A vacuum sucked up any silk that was left. I was carted to the recovery room, given grape juice until the bleeding lessened.

Mother met me in the waiting room. "Was it awful?"

I nodded.

"It's worse having a baby."

Neither of us knew that within a year, I'd be pregnant again.

I PUSHED BEA to her walk-in closet, a large room with floor-to-ceiling storage with a mix of shelves and wardrobe bars.

She scanned her wardrobe.

I sighed, resigned to the fact that Bea could spend an hour deciding what clothes to wear. She liked to rub the fabric, read tags, and discuss her clothing options. Then once the outfit was selected, the right shoes had to be chosen.

She pointed to black pants. I handed them to her.

"Bea, you know, when my mother was dying she visited a priest. I was thinking that she asked for absolution and he refused to give it to her."

She handed me back the pants.

"I didn't give it to her, either. You're more like a mother to me than she ever was."

"The blue pants, honey," she said. "Over there."

"These?" I handed her the pants.

"I love you, honey."

I leaned and we kissed.

"Bea?"

"Yes, honey."

"I did something so you wouldn't forget me."

"What's that?"

"I'll show you at breakfast."

"Don't hurry me. Hand me the other black pants."

At every meal, Bea sat and stared out her third-story window. Pine trees and hardwoods divided her yard from a ballfield. A hollow naturally formed in the branch of one of the trees. For a year, I had told her that something lived in the hollow and that we just hadn't seen it yet. She wasn't convinced. That morning, I made one stop before stepping on the elevator to her condo. I climbed her fence, scrambled up the tree, and put a gnome inside the hollowed-out limb.

"The usual this morning, Bea?" I asked, setting the lemon poppyseed muffin in front of her with a dab of cream cheese. "I have your bowl of grapefruit ready, too."

The gnome's hair was white under a bright red conical hat. He had dancing eyes with an overly large smile showing through his bushy beard.

Suddenly, Bea laughed and laughed. She laughed so hard that she started coughing.

I quickly grabbed for Kleenex.

She wiped her eyes. "I'm proud of you, honey." She chuckled. "You'll do well at the foundry."

After breakfast, Bea asked me to get the photo album off her bookshelf. "The one with my husband, honey."

Bea leafed slowly through the album. She stopped at the picture of a man in a military uniform, her bright red fingernails tapping the photo. "Isn't he handsome?" she said. "He was wounded at the very end of World War II, when his platoon was ordered to take a German unit making a last stand on a hill in Italy."

"My mother was in the Navy," I said, my gaze wandering around the room. "She assisted in the repatriation of World War II German refugees." I had no idea what that meant. My mother didn't talk about it. I now knew that I had never known my mother.

Mother was sitting in her bed at the Minneapolis VA Hospital. "You look awful in those clothes," she said when I knocked on her door and entered. "They make you look fat." Then she went on, "Margaret called and said that you brought everyone gifts back from Tonga. You know you can't buy your brothers' and sisters' love."

I stopped in her doorway. Her eyes were glassy, her head bald. I said in a flat voice, "Mom, I know you're dying and in pain. But I won't visit you if you're not nice to me."

Our eyes met. She opened her mouth, shut it. There was a glimmer in her eyes that told me she understood. "You can't be mean to me," I said.

After my thirty-day leave, I had returned to Tonga only to realize that I couldn't be an ocean away waiting for a phone call to tell me that my mother was dead. The cancer had spread to her bones. Bumps extruded from her head. I wanted to rub the largest one, but she batted my hand away.

"I asked your sisters if I should take treatment to extend my life," she said.

"HOW MUCH TIME, honey, before we have to leave for lunch?" Bea asked. "We don't want anyone waiting for us."

"An hour, sweetie."

The phone rang. I handed Bea the phone.

MOTHER LEFT THE HOSPITAL for the homestead. She called and asked me to come for a Labor Day celebration. "Everyone will be here."

After arriving, I sat outside their fifth-wheel camper at the picnic table and surveyed the countryside, just as she may have done the day she met my dad. It was peaceful, with the wind rustling through the trees. In May, when I first came home, the corn was a few inches high. It was now drying in the fields and within a month would be harvested. Shouts and laughter came from siblings. They were flying kites at the edge of a hay field. Margaret approached me at the picnic table. She lost her balance, then righted herself. She held a glass in her hand, careful not to spill a drop. Her voice slurred. "Thanks, Ann, for reporting the abuse. I don't know how it affected me, but I know it fucked me up." My two other sisters trailed behind her.

"Yeah, thanks," they chimed in.

Their words made me feel good, solid as the large oak tree, 150 years old, that stood steady and sure at the driveway entrance. Beyond the tree, across the road, was a hayfield, and above it a kite was flying—a simple, ordinary kite soaring above the rest and by itself.

At the end of the afternoon and before my siblings left, I drew near my mother. She was sitting in a lawn chair, her face weary. Her red lipstick had faded. She had taken off her brown floral-print headscarf. In a few weeks, she'd be reduced to nothing. I wondered if she'd die on my son's birthday. I realized now that for my son, the question of God may be more important than the question about who his mother was. I hugged my mother goodbye. This was as good as it was ever going to get.

A BOUQUET OF RED ROSES was in a vase on the dining room table. The front of the card had two teddy bears hugging. *I love you. Jody.*

"What are these for?" I pointed to the flowers.

She set the empty green recycling basket inside the closet. "You never gave up," she said. "That's what I admire about you. Whatever you set your sights on, you do."

Jody gave me cards and little presents to tell me how she felt about me. I had to refer to a plaque on the wall to get our anniversary date right. At this moment, all I could think of was how I felt stuck not having my own money. I didn't even realize it until I started working again. Now I would have choices. There was talk that a constitutional amendment to ban same-sex marriage would be on the ballot in November 2012. I wasn't sure that I wanted to be married to Jody.

Antonio and Crystel were in the front yard. Antonio was perched on an upper limb in the crabapple tree, knocking off pink blossoms. Crystel was tossing a rope up to him with no success.

Jody reached for a box of ring macaroni from the cupboards, put a pan of water on to boil. "I put the phone number by the flowers."

"What phone number?"

"The number from my old neighbors who adopted two daughters."

My heart beat faster. A rush of love for Jody warmed my body. Even though she might be afraid of the future, she came through for me. I moved school papers around on the table and found the number under Antonio's math homework. I stepped outside with my cell phone. The late May evening was warm. I smelled the fragrant mock orange shrub. I walked over to the corner of the house, where the shrub stood six feet tall. I pulled a branch down to smell the white flowers.

I was breathless when I came in the house. "Jody, they were just in Guatemala two weeks ago." I went on, "They've had four visits with their daughter's birth families." I bumped her shoulder by the sink. "They've been working with a group of four Guatemalan women who help adoptive families find the birth mothers."

At bedtime, I hugged Antonio and Crystel hard.

After I came to the living room, I sent an email to Susi at de Familia a Familia in Guatemala. Even though the adoption records had Jody listed as the birth mother, I signed my name and not hers. The next day, Susi emailed with a list of the documents she needed to start the birth search.

That evening, I opened the heavy lid of the lockbox and fingered through the adoption records. The rigid, thick, laminated Chain of Custody documents were easy to feel. I couldn't help but pull them out, look into the dark eyes of the birth mothers, and trace their faces.

I hesitated writing the check for over one thousand dollars for Crystel's birth mother search. Spending this money meant there were a lot of things our family would go without. This was one time that I didn't mind Antonio's reluctance to go first. We couldn't afford two searches at once. I put his documents back into the lockbox and put Crystel's paperwork in an envelope to take to work.

It was 6:00 a.m. in my human resources office when I checked my email. My skin tingled. Susi wrote that she had enough information and was ready to travel to San Miguel Petapa to locate Crystel's birth mom. I hugged myself. It was dreamlike. I didn't need to ask a judge for permission to search out her birth mom. I didn't need to go to a government building and request her records. How different this was from the United States. Within six weeks of my first contact with Susi, she was ready to meet the birth mother.

"Please send me a letter that I can give Mayra with ten photos of Crystel," she wrote.

I sent a text to Jody: "They found her. Call me."

I kicked off my street shoes, pushed them under my desk, and put on steel-toed shoes with metatarsals. Next, I slipped on a flame-retardant green jacket, my hard hat with earmuffs, and switched my eyeglasses for safety glasses. Right before I left my office, I stuffed my front jacket pocket with atomic fireballs from a candy jar on my desk.

The foundry was dimly lit and loud with the violent hammering of moving machinery. I followed the narrow walkway down a ramp, staying in the middle of the footpath. I kept my hands to my side or tucked in front of me. The burnt-toast smell and smoky darkness reminded me of the volcano at the base of Pacaya. I climbed a short ladder to the pouring deck and offered a fireball candy to a foundry guy.

"Good morning," I said.

He nodded, held out his gloved palm. The iron pourer had been at work for an hour. He was dressed in the same manner I was, except he was also wearing an aluminum apron, gloves, and chaps. I stepped back. The dinghy, a special ladle car, was riding the rails with molten iron. The transfer ladle poured 2,800-degree liquid iron into the casting ladle. Hot lava was being poured. Flames shot up when the pourer threw a small paper bag of alloy into the stream. I stepped back even further. This molten iron was hotter than lava. I was standing at the mouth of a volcano. The air was cloudy with smoke. I ran my tongue over my teeth, which were gritty with the black sand that permeated everything.

I walked through the foundry, hemmed in by fire and men, handing out fireballs. Once in a while I'd stop and make a note on a sheet of paper in my pocket. A new phone number, someone wanted a tax form, another wanted me to check how many vacation days he had left.

Back in my office, I took off the green jacket. Amid the fine black sand that coated my file cabinets, desk, and computer, I wrote this letter to Mayra.

Dear Mayra,

Your daughter, Crystel, would very much like to meet you.

She has asked, what do you think my mama will say when she first sees me?

I tell her, "Oh, she will say that you are beautiful, funny, and smart." Then she laughs.

Crystel likes to laugh. . . .

I told Mayra about Crystel attending a Spanish immersion school, learning piano, and playing soccer.

How should I sign the letter? Maybe Mayra didn't have any records that stated that Jody was the adopting mother, or maybe she doesn't remember Jody's name. I thought about our children. It was not worth complicating matters, as long as I was not totally invisible.

Love,
From her Mama in the United States,
Jody

My cell phone rang. It was Jody. It was the right decision to sign her name as the adopting mother, but I also refused to be invisible.

Later that evening, I picked out ten photos of Crystel from when she was an infant to the present day.

"Susi met Mayra," I texted Jody two weeks later.

That evening, crowded on our living room couch, the four of us looked hungrily at the forty photos Susi had emailed.

"See, Crystel. Susi is knocking on your birth mom's door. She lives right there." The door was turquoise blue. The next photo showed Mayra sitting at a table in a brown t-shirt with four of Crystel's siblings. Tears sat on Mayra's eyelids as she looked at a photo of Crystel. One sister had her hand covering her mouth, and the other had her eyes closed and was biting her lip. One sister was holding a baby. The next picture showed her sister taking her hand away from her mouth and placing it over her heart, and the sister with the baby had moved closer to the photo.

Tears flowed down my cheeks. Jody was crying, too. Antonio and Crystel's eyes were glued to the computer screen. I called up Susi's letter and read her words to everyone.

> I found Mayra home and some of her children. One of the girls opened the door and went to call her mother. When I told Mayra that I had photos for her from Crystel Rocio, she immediately invited me in and we sat down. The girls surrounded her and as soon as I gave her the photos, all the women started to cry. They cried a lot and Mayra's hands were visibly shaking. When I read your letter, they cried more. [. . .]
>
> Mayra's first words after listening to your letter were, "I think of her every day and we talk about her all the time. I was going through a big crisis at the time. I did not want to die without knowing about her. I prayed to hear from her and the Lord answered me. We never lost our faith that we would see her again."

"You're much loved, Crissy," I said.
Crystel wriggled closer to my side.

> Her sister Astrid said, "Although we were very young, I still remember. It was very painful for all of us when my mom arrived home without her.

I stopped for a moment, thought of my brother Johnny, who was five years old. "When's the baby coming, Ann, when's

the baby coming?" How disappointed he was when no baby
came home.

Even now, leaving Johnny was one of the hardest things I
ever did. I had been to the farm for what I knew to be the last
time. When I was getting into my car, he ran out, hugging me,
not wanting to let go. I didn't want to leave him, either. Leave
him to our mother. But it was clear—it was my life or his. Before he died, he'd tell me how I treated him like a son.

I continued to read out loud the letter from Susi.

> Mayra remembered exactly the date of Crystel's birth.
> Most birth mothers do not, not for lack of interest but
> because dates are usually not important. She named her
> Crystel Rocio. Crystel because: "I felt she was a little
> fragile thing as crystal, and Rocio ('dew' in English), be-
> cause as I was walking the day I gave birth to her, it was
> cloudy and it had rained during the night, and I saw the
> leaves with drops of dew on them." [. . .]
> I asked if she had any questions.
> She looked at me and said, "I have so many questions."

Antonio slid off the back of the couch, landed with a
thump on the floor. Our eyes met.

"As soon as we have enough money," I said.

About two and a half months later we had the funds for
Rosa's search. I sent Susi a letter to give to Rosa and ten photos
of Antonio. She located Rosa in Rabinal. Forty-four pictures
detailed her trip.

Just as before, Antonio, Crystel, Jody, and I gathered in
the living room. This time Crystel laid on the back of the
couch and Antonio sat between Jody and me.

Rosa had a string of red beads around her neck. She had a strong Mayan face and her dark brown eyes were wet with tears. She was wearing a colorful wraparound skirt with a black blouse and was leaning against a post under a tin roof.

"Remember, Antonio, the long drive to your village, during our Guatemala trip when you were seven?" I said. A photo showed a paved road leaving Rabinal, climbing a high ridge with a green, hilly view to the left into mountain ranges. "Should we read the letter?"

[. . .] I opened the envelope and handed Rosa the photos you sent. She looked at them and started crying and she blessed me saying that she has been waiting to have news from Antonio for a long time. She mentioned how well and handsome he is and it touched my heart when she asked me if she could keep one photo. [. . .] She was happy to know all of them were for her.

I asked if she named Antonio and she said no, that she wanted to name him Juan José (Juan to honor her father and José to honor her grandfather), but the adoption people named him Antonio.

I paused, then continued to read out loud.

"I want to thank Antonio for the photos and to tell him that I hope I will be able to see him again one day; I would like very much that and I would like him to forgive me for letting him go. I hope he will give me the opportunity to explain everything. I love him very much."

After the kids went to bed, it was just me and Jody. She was sitting on the floor and as usual her back was to the heat register, even though the heat wasn't on. The house was quiet. A loneliness was settling in. Though my partner was in the same room, she might as well have not been there. I opened the refrigerator. Closed it. Went downstairs to bed.

THE NEXT DAY was ductile day at the foundry. When greater strength was needed than that provided by gray iron castings, ductile castings were made. Each department in the foundry smelled a little different than the other, depending how close or how far away you were from the volcano.

Antonio and Crystel were stronger because they had seen the pictures of each of their birth moms, but what if they hugged them, smelled the scent of their necks, and looked into their eyes?

I walked through the cooling shed, floating my hand above the hot, dirty castings held in metal tubs. Heat emanated from the casts. *I didn't want to die without knowing about Crystel. I prayed to hear from her and the Lord answered me. We never lost our faith that we would see her again.* Inside the door of the finishing department I heard hammers banging, the whir of grinders, and cutoff blades. After castings were shot-blasted, they rumbled down a conveyor to be sorted and hauled away to snag-grinding workstations, where they were hoisted up to a worktable. Most employees were wearing full respirator masks. I walked back through the molten metal area, keeping an eye open for any drink cans. Moisture mixed with molten iron explodes, the same way molten rock under great pressure in a magma chamber results in a volcanic eruption. *I would like Antonio to forgive me for letting him go.*

THREE MONTHS LATER, I sat down to our company-assigned table at an American Foundry Society dinner meeting. I was thinking about Jody. I ran out of the house without saying goodbye. Even though we had been sleeping in the same bed, it had been months since we had been intimate.

The man seated next to me had been married for forty years and was ten years older than me. Eugene touched me on my back, pointed to the podium. His contact caused my pulse to race. He was not a man I was normally attracted to. He was short, heavyset, and nearly bald. I sat with my right leg over my left, reached down to straighten my sock. Above my ankle was an outline of a red-and-yellow sun with Antonio's and Crystel's names. Inside the sun was the Chinese symbol for love. Jody had the same tattoo. We got the tattoos on a trip to Mexico. Jody had organized the romantic getaway, which was something she hadn't ever done before. Usually it was me who planned all of our adventures. She knew our relationship was in trouble. She could sense my growing angst. She wasn't even sure that I'd come on this trip that she had planned. I wasn't ready to totally give up. She loved me.

"Foundry workers die at a rate more than twice that of workers in other manufacturing industries," said the speaker. "Third-degree burns, crushed limbs, and amputations are common. Extreme noise, heat, dust, and fumes are facts of foundry work." He went on to say that only the desperate sought work at a foundry; the word "desperate" stuck in my head. I worked my chair to be closer to Eugene.

The speaker said excessive heat in the foundry could cause headaches, confusion, fainting, convulsions, even coma. I hadn't had a drink in more than thirty-four years, yet I was intoxicated being near Eugene. When it was time to go, I stumbled getting to my feet and he steadied me.

Nine months later, I sat in Eugene's office, which was situated on the manufacturing floor in-between the melt and the mould departments. I had become accustomed to the slamming of air-driven hammers and presses, the combustion roar of the three blast furnaces, and the massive equipment that shudders and shakes. During lunch, Eugene and I walked hand in hand to the local park. He asked me about my past.

"It's complicated," I said. "What my dad and brothers did, you are fixing."

That's what I thought at first. Now I know that when I feel safe with a man, his love can touch the depth of my pain, the rawness of betrayal. When I was nine years old, Simon penetrated me after saying he wouldn't. Then other brothers followed. Then my dad touched my breasts. I was a nine-year-old girl who wanted to be loved. The part of me that was still nine years old felt safe with Eugene. Eugene was my brothers and my father and his love a balm to that deep betrayal. Because a sexual relationship with Eugene at the onset was unconceivable to both of us, it allowed us to become emotionally close in a very short time. What Eugene saw was a married lesbian with two children. What I saw was a short, heavyset man who was in his sixties and who had been married for over forty years.

Jody saw it for what it was. On a walk, she asked me, "Did you kiss him?"

I gave her a sideways look. "Are you sure . . . you want to ask me that?"

Color drained from her face. She stopped walking. "Yes."

I answered with a small nod.

Her mouth opened, but no words formed. She closed them with a pinch and stomped ahead of me.

The question that I eventually would have to face was whether I would let my relationship with Jody go in order to chase a love that gave this nine-year-old girl such comfort. And if not Eugene, would it be another man? Or would I be able to accept that there wasn't going to be a do-over for this nine-year-old?

WHEN I WAS TWENTY-FIVE years old, I drove to our unoccupied farm in Wisconsin with my Annie doll, a doll I bought in my early twenties. She reminded me of when I was little, with her blue denim jumper and braided yellow pigtails. When I arrived at the empty farm, I placed Annie on the grass behind the old house where Simon first penetrated me. A wispy, trailing cloud passed over. "Your body is yours," I said. "I'm sorry you were hurt. I love you, Annie." Tears streamed down my face as I moved to the crawlspace in the old house, reached by climbing a ladder from the outside. I laid Annie down on the dusty floor. I picked her up and cradled her, murmuring softly.

I laid her down in my old bedroom, in the potato bin in the basement, in the haymow, in front of the cow stantions, and in the cornfield. Then I moved to the old silo. The rusty iron rungs were secure in the face of the cement. I stuffed the cloth doll in the front of my shorts and climbed. My breathing became labored. I looked down, looked up. I climbed the next step. My breathing frightened me. I wasn't used to being scared. I had climbed this silo dozens of times as a child. There were three steps left. *Beth, you don't need to do this. You have nothing to prove. No one is chasing you. You aren't a failure if you don't go to the top.* I gazed out over the farm and at the intersection of Highway 63 and Highway 72, the creek bed, and the still fields. This used to be my world. It wasn't anymore. I began my climb down.

At the base of the silo was the collar of a broken wine bottle. I fingered the sharp edges, remembering how my siblings and I would throw any empties we found against the barn and silo, our ears poised for the delicious explosion of glass hitting cement.

Inside the old house, the house we lived in until I was nine, I found an empty Bell glass canning jar. Mother canned sauerkraut, pickles, and tomatoes. I placed the jagged wine head, my dad, the violence, the fights, the touching of my breasts into the jar. I was a real girl; the sexual abuse happened to me. No one could tell me that I made it up. The twisted silver table fork that I dropped into the jar was my mother standing over a long kitchen table full of children eating birthday cake, her little girl with blonde pigtails standing on her chair to make herself as big as her brothers. The yellow marble were those brothers, my heroes, whom I loved. Small squares of tile that I ripped up from the kitchen floor and scraps of green-and-red wallpaper I tore off the wall was the home I grew up in. In the yard, I picked up three different-shaped pinecones and a dried seed pod and carefully placed me with the items.

Smelling smoke, I lifted my nose to the air. The smell was the same as it was in fourth grade, when the scent of grass burning wafted into St. Francis Church as we schoolchildren knelt, stood, knelt, stood, and sung throughout Mass. A fire engine siren sounded. I followed the direction of the siren. Our farm was four miles to the east.

On the playground during lunch, one of my classmates said, "Hey, Ann, that was your barn that burned down."

"No, it didn't," I replied. "It wasn't ours." I covered my face, ran to the corner of the school building.

He shouted after me, "Yeah, it was. I heard it downtown, when I was with my mom at the dentist."

I asked Thomas at afternoon recess. "Is it true?" I asked.

"I don't know," he said angrily. He walked away from me to play football with the boys.

David, Thomas, and I pushed out the bus door. We raced down the gravel road to our mailbox and up the hill, slowing to a walk. Neighbors and farmers stood with shovels and hoses, turning over smoldering wood bits.

Hay combustion was the story our parents told. It happens sometimes, you know? Hay, heat, light.

A siren in the far distance brought me back to the Bell canning jar I held. I visually measured the contents. Yes, this was a compilation of my life.

Back on the road, I turned right at the bank, heading to the doctor's office. I waited for Dr. Klaas in the same examination room in which he diagnosed my pregnancy, the same room he stripped skin off my back.

"Why did you ask me when I was fourteen if I was pregnant by my brothers?" I asked.

"I ask everyone that." His tall frame filled the doorway.

I didn't believe him.

I had one last appointment before leaving Ellsworth. I met with the high-school principal, who was now the superintendent. I apologized for the school fights, the mice on chairs, the throwing of eggs down the hallway, the jumping out of windows, the school bathroom fire . . . yeah, *that* fire . . . in tenth grade.

It was perfect. AES. The smoky gray initials looked down at me from the tenth-grade bathroom ceiling. *Cool. No one will know they're mine but me. Ann Elizabeth Smith. I own them. Mine.*

"Hey Ann," Judy whispered from the stool. She sat with her back against the partition, took a deep drag of her Marlboro, held the smoke in her lungs, and then blew a spectacular O. She'd been humming the lyrics to "Smokin' in the Boys Room" by Brownsville Station.

I lay sprawled, perched on top of the stall. "Yeah, what?" I flicked my lighter, darkened the "E" on the ceiling and moved back to the "A."

She hummed, *Teacher, don't you fill me up with your rules.* "I dare you to light a fire." *Everybody knows that smokin' ain't allowed in school.* Dropped her butt in the toilet.

There was a loud hiss.

"What?" I lengthened the right leg of the "A" to be as long as the other.

She rested a foot on the toilet seat. "I'll stand watch outside. You roll the paper towel down. Light it. Take off."

"What?"

"Come on. Nobody will know." She sashayed out of the stall, singing as she went, "Checkin' out the halls, makin' sure the coast is clear. Lookin' in the stalls, nah, there ain't nobody here. Dah ta da ta da ta. To get caught would surely be the death of us all."

"Okay, okay. You better make sure no one is out there."

Judy left the bathroom. I clambered down.

She opened the door an inch. "Hurry up, Ann! Hurry! Classes are over."

I rushed to the wall dispenser next to the hand basin. Quickly, I unrolled the paper to my chest. I held the paper with my left hand. Rested the Zippo against my jeans with my right. Dragged it backward. The lid flipped open. I pushed the Zippo forward to strike the wheel. Set the flame to the paper. Ran.

"WHAT DO YOU MEAN you did it on a dare?" the school-appointed psychologist asked me.

"I did it on a dare."

"Tell me why you really did it," he said.

Fuck you, asshole. Think I don't know what you're doing?
"I did it on a dare," I repeated.

He studied me.

I was slouched in my chair. I wore jeans ripped at the knees and a t-shirt.

He lifted his hand, removed his glasses, and twirled them.

I noticed how the white rubber bumper on my left sneaker was dirty and smudged. The right sneaker also had a splatter, a tinge of brown. I must had spilled chili from lunch when I got jostled carrying my tray. I looked out the small window in his office.

He leaned toward me. "Your house burned down, didn't it?"

"What!" I straightened in the chair.

"Your house burned down, right?"

"I wasn't even there! Look at the records! I was in school!" I grabbed the armrests.

"How old were you?"

"I wasn't even there! Look at the school records!" But in an instant, I jumped on the cylinder. Saw how I could have skipped third period, poured gas around the house, and then snuck back into school by lunchtime.

"Is there anything you want to tell me?"

Fuck you, you asshole. Who's going to take care of my sisters? I'm already damaged.

"Then we're finished. I'm going to talk to your parents."

Choking back tears, I pushed past my parents in the waiting room. "He thinks I burnt the house down!" I said, my red-hot eyes boring into them.

I ran to the car. Once inside, I broke down sobbing. I didn't trust that my parents would set the record straight. I'd be the fall guy for the house and barn burning, too. Maybe I'd get sent away.

THAT EVENING AT BEDTIME, Crystel asked her nightly question, "Mama Beth, what was your most embarrassing moment today?"

I told her about Eugene. "Crystel, I told him that he was my BFF."

She clasped her hands together. "What did he say, Mama?"

"What's that? Big. Fat. Friend?"

Crystel laughed loudly. I tried to quiet her because I was sure that Antonio and Jody could hear her in his bedroom.

"What's going on in here?" Jody said, opening the door.

I gave Crystel a stern look. "We're just having fun."

Crystel stifled a giggle.

PART
SIX

PART

SIX

DRAGGING OUR LUGGAGE TO THE INTERNATIONAL AIRLINE counter, we stuck together, the four of us. The dark blue trailing suitcase tipped over. It was unwieldy, bulging with gifts for Crystel's birth family. Gifts for Antonio's birth family were packed tightly in its matching, smaller version. Bracing the baggage with my foot, I yanked and pulled it upright. I was overdressed because I didn't like to be cold. The exertion of struggling with luggage caused me to perspire. I tugged at my layers, pulling them away from my clammy skin. Antonio reached for one end of the large suitcase and slid the baggage to the counter. Jody tucked her short brown hair behind her ears.

"You all going to Guatemala?" asked the attendant.

"Yes, we are," we answered in unison, bellying up to the counter.

Unlike our first trip, when we adopted the children, Jody and I had split up the passports and airline tickets. I pulled out mine and Crystel's. I touched my ear. It was naked. Jody and I had taken off all of our jewelry the night before. My ring finger was also bare.

Crystel had a window seat, Antonio the middle, and Jody next to him. I sat one row behind. When we were in the air and above the clouds, Crystel shouted. "Mama Beth, Mama Beth."

I took off my headset.

She was kneeling on the seat, pointing. She was so excited that her finger wavered. "See the rabbit, see the rabbit."

A sea of clouds was out the window. "I do, Crystel. Way over there in the far right corner."

"Yes, Mama."

"We found her, didn't we, honey."

"Yes, we did, Mama, but what if I can't remember all my brothers' and sisters' names?"

"I'll be there, Crystel."

She nodded.

The airline stewardess walked down the aisle offering alcohol, soda, water, and coffee. "What beer do you have?" I asked. I listened to the choices. "Henieken, please."

Months earlier, not unlike Step Four of the Alcoholics Anonymous program—make a searching and fearless inventory of ourselves—I evaluated my life. I questioned everything. I wasn't sure that I was going to stay in my relationship with Jody. My relationship with Eugene had awoken my longing to be with a man. It seemed like for me to have the most in life, I needed to be with a woman. But now I wasn't so sure. Eugene provided me with the safety to explore my feelings of love and desire. Maybe I could be with a man. It was also natural for me to analyze my thirty-four years of sobriety. I concluded that when I was nineteen, going into treatment was my way out of my family. Alcoholics Anonymous saved my life. It taught me how to live. It was my family for twenty years. Even so, I didn't think I was an alcoholic. I told Jody I wanted to go to a restaurant and order a drink. After a pause, she told me that she did, too. She had been examining her life, as well.

One airline seat in front of me, Jody reached for her glass of wine.

In the lobby of Hotel Grand Tikal Futura, Jody, Antonio, Crystel, and I bunched to the right of the reception area. It was ten in the morning. Two hotel clerks dressed in pressed black pants, white shirts, and black blazers were checking people in.

Rosa and Susi were late. The four of us stood and waited, expecting them any moment.

Towering glass architecture provided plenty to look at. But we kept our eyes on the entrance.

A short Guatemalan woman stepped across the large lobby. Her hair was pulled back with a wide, black, crocheted headband. She had on a red terry jacket over a light blue blouse. She was wearing jeans and sandals. The woman smiled shyly at us, tears flowing down her cheeks.

I had a lump in my throat. "Rosa?"

Antonio stepped forward. Rosa enveloped him in her arms and spoke to him in Spanish.

Jody and I started to cry. Rosa kissed Antonio on the cheek and held him close to her. I didn't try to wipe my tears away. They were so plentiful.

Susi was suddenly beside us holding Rosa's two-year-old daughter, Ani's, hand. Ani's hair was bundled with pink barrettes. She was wearing a pink Princess Ariel shirt and pink pants. She reminded me of Crystel at that age.

Jody and I took turns hugging Susi and Rosa.

We walked very slowly to the pool area. There were two connected, indoor, heated pools. We drifted to the far left corner. Two tables were squeezed together. I set the suitcase on one and took out three tropical bubble bottles.

"Antonio, show your sister how to blow bubbles."

He blew bubbles toward Ani.

Ani smiled and slid off Rosa's lap, holding her hand out.

Antonio handed her the wand, then set the bubbles on the table in front of her.

For the next fifteen minutes we watched Antonio, Crystel, and Ani blow bubbles and giggle.

I encouraged Antonio and Crystel to show Ani what we brought her. We all laughed when Antonio blew up a beach ball for Ani and she pointed to her shirt, jumping up and down. Princess Ariel was depicted on both.

Antonio sat next to Rosa and showed her a photo book. As he turned each page to tell her what was in the photo, Susi translated. He handed the book to Rosa. Her cheeks were puffy and red. Both Rosa and Antonio had full lips, similar eyes and eyebrows. Both were reserved and shy. Rosa handed Antonio three weavings that his grandmother made. She explained that the cotton was obtained at the end of winter, then dyed in white or coffee color before it was made into the colorful hues.

Antonio, Crystel, and Ani changed into their swimsuits. Our tables were next to the pool for children. In the pool, the children tossed the beach ball back and forth. When Ani's throw went to the other side of the pool, Antonio retrieved it for her.

We adults pushed one table to the side and maneuvered our chairs to be close to each other. Jody and I sat facing Rosa. Susi stood behind her and interpreted.

Rosa told us her father died in 1982, during the Civil War, and her mother was left to raise seven children on her own. Her mother could not provide for all, so she gave Rosa to an aunt when she was five years old. Her aunt treated her very badly, so Rosa ran away back to her mom's house. She had to get a job cleaning houses in Rabinal at age nine to help with money. She never went to school and, therefore, could barely read or write. Antonio was the same age that Rosa was when she had to start work.

Susi and Rosa talked back and forth in Spanish. Rosa said that Antonio had a sister who was three years older, and she lived with her mother. There was also an older brother who was eighteen, but Rosa didn't have a relationship with him. He lived with his paternal grandparents. She was fifteen years old when she gave birth to him, and because she could not provide for him, his grandparents took him away from her. She explained that was why it was important to her to have a good relationship with Antonio.

I took several short breaths. "Susi, would you translate for me?" My eyes clouded over. I told Rosa that I was just like her. Tears spilled from my eyes. I gulped for air. "I had a baby boy when I was a teenager," I said. "I gave him up for adoption." Rosa began to cry.

"That's . . . why . . . it was important for me . . . to have you meet Antonio," I said. "I know what it's like to give up a baby."

Tears poured down both our faces.

Rosa grasped my hands, held them in hers. She pulled me in for a hug. We sobbed together.

"I promise . . . to care for . . ." I couldn't go on, but then I did. ". . . and love . . . Antonio."

Ani was calling for her mama to bring a towel. Antonio and Crystel were also getting out of the pool. Lunch came. Susi carefully wrapped the leftover bread and bits of chicken in a napkin. Rosa put it in her purse.

Before our visit was over, I asked Susi if Rosa needed any help with monthly groceries.

Rosa said, "No. I don't want Antonio to feel as if I have sold him."

"No, no, Rosa," we said. "Antonio knows you love him."

Still she insisted she was fine, but if she needed help, she'd ask.

We said our goodbyes at the cab outside of the hotel. Susi checked with the cab driver to make sure he drove to Rosa's zone. Rosa lived in the poorest and most dangerous zone of Guatemala City. Often, taxis wouldn't go there.

Rosa and Ani were in the backseat of the cab. Our suitcase full of gifts for them was in the trunk. The necklace Antonio gave to Rosa was around her neck, the mother and baby dangling above her heart. The white gold pendant expressed one of the strongest bonds in nature: a mother's love for her child.

At dinner that evening in the hotel, Antonio asked me why I was crying with Rosa.

"I had a baby boy just like Rosa did," I said again, although we had already spoken of this. My voice was tearful. "I gave him up for adoption, too, remember?"

"That must have been hard," Antonio said. "Did you ever meet him?"

"No, sweetie, that's why it was so important to me that you meet Rosa."

He smiled. "Thanks, Mama."

The next morning, we arrived at La Aurora Guatemalan Zoo before it opened. A white van was parked under a Ceiba tree, with a group of fifteen Guatemalan men and women of all ages milling about.

"That's them," I said.

There was some doubt in our car.

"No, that's them," I insisted. "Crystel, let's go meet your mama."

Mayra had on a gray short-sleeved shirt with blue jeans and tennis shoes. She walked toward us. I knew it was her from photos. Her cheeks were shiny with tears. She pulled Crystel into her, cradling her left hand on Crystel's head and her right hand across her back. Then she took her hand off Crystel's head and put them both around her, embracing her even closer. Crystel was smiling, looking downward, with her arms tucked to her body. Brothers, sisters, and an aunt started touching her hair, arms, and face. Crystel's youngest brother, Christian, who was seven, stood next to her and took her hand. He posed for a picture with Crystel, positioning his head in the crook of her chin. Christian would stay at her side for most of the visit.

Susi hadn't arrived. I introduced all of us, then asked our driver to bring out the large blue suitcase and place it on the ground. First I took out the remote control car and mimicked an engine revving, making people laugh. Crystel's nephew, who was two, took the car and maneuvered it in the empty parking lot. Next I brought out a boy's athletic red-and-black zipper sweatjacket, held it up to her oldest brother, and shook my head no. It went down the line of four brothers until we reached Christian, who had remained at Crystel's side. He immediately put on the jacket and didn't take it off throughout the day, even though it warmed up considerably.

Her oldest brother asked what we brought him. I picked up a ladies' blouse out of the suitcase and raised my eyebrows. There was much laughter.

Inside the suitcase was a stack of school pictures of Crystel. I handed them to her. She handed one to each member of her family. I breathed a sigh of relief that we had brought

enough. I handed Crystel the brooch for Mayra. She gave it
to Mayra, and her oldest daughter helped pin it on.

Crystel was wearing a white top with large pink butterflies. Someone placed over her head a necklace of pink and
white shells. Another person put a folded fleece blanket in her
hands. And then her mother placed a necklace with a locket
around her neck. She explained that inside the locket was a
picture of her and an empty place for a photo of Crystel.

A bouquet of multicolored roses was placed in Jody's
hands, then a single red rose, then a bundle of floral fabric.
Jody's face turned pale. She wasn't smiling or frowning. She
moved the bouquet of flowers and cradled them on her left
side, held tight to the red rose in her left finger, and grasped
the fabric with her left hand. On her right shoulder hung a
large bag that held our jackets, which we had already shed.

I leaned in, expecting Jody to acknowledge me.

Mayra was expressing her thanks to Jody for loving her
daughter and caring for her. Jody's eyes were teary. She listened quietly to Mayra's praise her for how tall Crystel was,
how pretty she was, how smart she must be.

Jody didn't glance at me. I swallowed hard.

Susi had arrived and repeated what Mayra had said in English. Mayra told Jody thanks for the photos and the nice letter.
She could tell that Crystel had a sense of humor like all of her
sons and daughters. They liked to laugh and laugh, she said.

When Jody turned toward me, she gazed to my side and
didn't see me.

Tears welled up in my eyes and my chest ached. I was
afraid I'd start crying. I busied myself returning items to the
suitcase. Just as it would have been so very simple for my
mother to stop my brothers' abuse, it would have been so sim-

ple for Jody to acknowledge me. All she had to do was to pull me aside and tell me that she saw what was going on—she was being recognized as Crystel's mother. She could have even done it with a loving glance, a warm hug, a touch. I couldn't be with someone who wasn't present for me, who was like the family I grew up in. I wouldn't be invisible.

Antonio was standing apart from the group. I walked to him, gave him a hug, and asked how he was doing.

"Okay, Mama."

His eyes were a deep brown. I gave him another squeeze. "Crystel helped you yesterday playing with your sister. Today's your turn."

He nodded, fiddled with a rock he picked up. I observed the group of people flocking around Jody. "That's what family does; they are there for each other." My throat and lungs hurt. "I love you, buddy."

When family wasn't there for you, you figured out what you needed to do for yourself.

Susi ushered us to the entrance of the zoo. Jody didn't move. Antonio put his arm in hers and escorted her to the admissions area. I ignored my heartbreak, set my jaw, and fixed my thoughts on what I needed to do to recognize myself as Crystel's mother. I put the question on the cylinder, ran it through a list of possibilities, fastened onto a solution.

Once we were in the queue, I pulled out of the line and took pictures of different groups, cajoling them to pose together. First, I had all nine of Mayra's children line up from oldest to youngest, with Crystel in the spot that she held in the family. Age twenty-three, twenty-two, twenty, eighteen, sixteen, fifteen, twelve, nine, and seven. Girl, boy, girl, girl, boy, boy, boy, Crystel, boy. Christian leaned his head on

Crystel's shoulder. In the next picture, the twenty-three-year-old had her two-year-old son join the photo, and her oldest brother beckoned his girlfriend to come with their baby. Much was made about Crystel having a new niece or nephew soon as the third-oldest girl, who was eighteen, was seven months pregnant. I handed my camera to Susi and took Mayra by the hand. I asked Jody and Crystel to join us. I put my hand around Mayra's shoulder, Jody stood on the other side of her, and Crystel stood a little in front of the three of us, just like it should be. All the moms together. Then I called Antonio over and another photo was snapped, with my left arm around Mayra and my right arm around Antonio.

There was one more photo that I knew I must have. A person who wasn't being seen, who must be acknowledged. He wasn't invisible to me.

A large man who had followed us remained on the fringes of the circle. He was important to the family, holding the baby, carrying bags, and staying close if called upon. I deduced that he was Mayra's boyfriend, though he hadn't been introduced. I asked Mayra and him to stand together. I took a picture. Then I asked Crystel, him, and Mayra to stand together and snapped another photo. I would recognize him. After all, it was so easy to do. After I finished, I handed Jody the camera, my expression stony.

Considered to be one of the best zoos in Central America, La Aurora Zoo has 100 different species and almost 1,000 animals. There were several exhibit areas, including the African savanna, the Asian subcontinent, the Mesoamerican tropics, and a farm. Our group leisurely walked down the park paths.

Mayra insisted on carrying Jody's bag for her.

It was toward the end of our zoo visit, at the aviary section, when Susi pulled me aside.

"I hope you don't mind. Mayra asked who you were. I told her that you were a good friend," she said in a gentle tone. She added, "I'm sorry."

"No, no, Susi," I said. I waved my hands in front of me. "It's okay." My chin trembled. "I don't want to cause trouble. Really, it's okay."

My heart was breaking because even this woman saw me. But my partner?

"When are you going to tell Mayra about your baby that you gave up in adoption?" asked Susi.

Crystel was mingling with her brothers and sisters. The group was focused on a peacock fanning its iridescent blue-green tail. "Crystel asked me not to tell that story," I said. "It upsets her when I cry."

"No, no. You must tell Mayra."

Already, I felt the tears. "Can you tell her for me?" I said.

"No. You must tell her in your words. I will interpret."

Crystel was walking toward the spectacled owl exhibit. Jody was standing in front of the Scarlet Macaw cage. The large red, yellow, and blue parrot was captivating. I bit my lower lip.

Mayra was speaking to her sister. I tapped her on the shoulder. "Mayra," I said. "Could I talk to you?"

She stepped closer to me. "Yes?"

"I want to tell you that I gave up a baby in adoption just like you." I couldn't hold in my tears and I started to cry. "That's why it was important for Jody and me to bring Crystel to meet you." At this, I started sobbing.

Mayra also sobbed. She reached to stroke my hair. Her voice cracked with emotion.

"Mayra is thanking you for loving her daughter," Susi said.

I laid a hand over my heart.

EPILOGUE

EPILOGUE

FLOWERS HAD OPENED TO THEIR UTMOST BLOOMS AND spread their green leaves their widest. Bees darted for nectar, dragonflies with iridescent wings dropped to the swimming pool for a quick drink. Butterflies watched from the fringes of the yard. It was a lovely day for a wedding.

Crystel, in a sleeveless black-and-white-striped dress, stepped slowly forward around the swimming pool. She moved as if to kneel and her hemline skirt opened, exposing her long brown legs. She carefully laid white rose petals on the pool decking. Crystel had always wanted to be a flower girl.

Jody and I were married for the first time on this very day twelve years earlier. It wasn't legal then. When we looked at our wedding album through the years, Crystel couldn't understand why she and Antonio weren't in the wedding photos. She recognized our backyard, our pool, and many of the seventy-five guests. "Because you weren't born yet," I told her. Since joining us as infants, Antonio and Crystel had doubled our blessings and our lives had grown exponentially. Today, our wedding would be legal and one hundred and fifty guests were honoring us with their presence.

In the audience were my Tae Kwon Do brothers. I sparred with these men weekly. Like me, they were also black belts.

After Antonio and Crystel became black belts, I, too, joined Tae Kwon Do. I loved feeling as if I could defend myself. I loved having men in my life who I felt close to. I loved having brothers.

Her smile wide, Crystel dipped again, allowing velvety white rose petals to spill gently from her hand. A scent of honey drifted up as she reached into her basket for more petals.

"I Choose You" a song by Sara Bareilles, was playing.

A dragonfly landed on a rock in the garden to bask in the afternoon sun. Twelve years earlier and again today, Jody and I had a dragonfly printed on our wedding program. In many parts of the world, dragonflies symbolize change and self-realization. For Jody and me, the dragonfly meant that we were willing to do our personal work.

At the hotel in Guatemala, I said to Jody, through a veil of tears, "You didn't see me. My family growing up didn't see me, either. I was invisible."

First her silence, then her blank, pale face affirmed her words. "I didn't know. You acted more like the mom than I did. I was trying to figure out how to be included. And then, when, finally, I was going to approach Mayra to talk to her, you were telling her about giving up your baby."

Jody and I continued to talk after we returned to Minnesota. She understood that I wanted to be the most important person in her life, to be considered before her biological family and to be placed in front of her work. She began turning down her family's invitations when they conflicted with our family activities. And when they didn't, she checked with me anyway. At night she shut off her computer and joined me on the couch.

Bareilles sang, "We are not perfect, we'll learn from our mistakes, and as long as it takes, I will prove my love to you."

I had made mistakes, too. I realized I had love in the palm of my hands with Jody as a partner. I felt her love. I knew that with my past, I would always need to work at showing that I loved her. It was me who asked her to marry.

The dragonfly lifted up from the rock, glided through the air, then changed direction swiftly and was gone.

Our wedding song continued, "I am not scared of the elements, I am underprepared, but I am willing, and even better, I get to be the other half of you." Jody's enduring love provided the space for me to fall in love with her all over again. I would strive to love her fully for the rest of my days.

Crystel laid rose petals at the entrance of our gazebo. She set her flower basket on a table and walked toward us. Antonio stepped forward, formally offered Crystel his arm. He was wearing a pinstripe vest and dress pants. Crystel locked her left arm with his. She looked downward and smiled shyly. Antonio was also in bare feet as he escorted Crystel midway around the pool to a bench. They would both sit and wait for their moms. Together the four of us would walk to the gazebo, our wedding chapel.

"I will become yours and you will become mine," Bareilles sang.

My wedding dress was sky blue, sleeveless, floor length, with a swoop back. It brought out the blue in my eyes and matched my toenails. Jody's dress had the same design, but was champagne. Her left arm was draped softly around mine.

Masses of bright yellow cornflowers called Golden Glow were in full bloom several feet above our head. Barefoot, I felt the softness of the rose petals under my feet. Our guests came into view. Words by Scott Russell Sanders were printed on our wedding program: "To be centered . . . means to have a home territory, to be attached in a web of relationships with other people, to value common experience, and to recognize that one's life rises constantly from inward depths."

Sunlight bounced off the pool and in the reflected light I saw her. The old woman, a *curasera*, a traditional Kachiquel Mayan healer from a remote village in the highlands of Guatemala. She wore a purple wrapped headscarf, a blue blouse that was hand-woven on a back-strap loom, and a skirt with *ikat* patterns woven into the textile. She was small, just a little over five feet, with coppery skin. Her dark brown eyes were set above high cheekbones and a prominent nose. I remembered how I stooped to enter the dark smoky cave that barely fit the old woman and me. The circular-domed *temascal*, a type of sweat lodge, was constructed from volcanic rock and cement. To produce the heat, volcanic stones were heated with a wood fire near the wall. My eyes burned from the leftover wood smoke. The old woman dipped cloth in warm water. I laid on a slab bench and shut my eyes. I was in my mother's womb, being washed from head to toe. The mother of all mothers was cleansing my mind, body, and spirit with a fusion of water and fire. From where I had once come, I had returned to heal myself. The old woman spoke a constant stream of Kachiquel, none of which I understood, yet her healing touch was unmistakable. Blood came to my head, my heartbeat quickened, and I was at peace.

Bareilles continued, "I choose you, I choose you, I choose you."

Antonio and Crystel kept their eyes focused on Jody and me. We walked arm in arm to join them. I now knew the answer to my questions, "How long do Antonio and Crystel have to belong to us to be a part of our family, to be from our family? If they were always from Guatemala, would they always be displaced people? Never truly be at home?"

Antonio and Crystel were ours from the very beginning. Choices were made long before any of us were born into this world. And yet, it wasn't destiny. All along the way, I made conscious choices to have this life. My greatest want was for my children to grow up without abuse and to witness what that looked like. It looked beautiful, strong, and free. I was healed through mothering them. I regarded my children leaning forward in their seats, ready to stand. I saw two amazing young people, self-possessed, confident, and full of grace.

OUR VOWS HAD been said, the first dance waltzed, the wedding dinner eaten, and the three-tier buttercream cake cut. Before the final farewell, Jody and I stepped up on the diving board above the pool, held hands, looked out at our future, and jumped.

Reading Guide Questions

- Why does the author begin her story with traveling with her partner to adopt children? What do we learn from the early scenes about the author's life?

- Although the author's mother was a social worker and her father a chemical dependency counselor, they ignored what was happening in their family. Discuss the family dynamic that might lead to this type of behavior.

- What does the book say about the origins of incest? About its consequences? Its possible prevention?

- Did *House of Fire* change the way you think of your own childhood?

- When you were a child, were there any adults you could turn to no matter what, or were you on your own?

- What did the author's parents teach her about the roles of men and women? Who were your most powerful role models? What did they teach you about the world?

- The author proved to be a survivor. Where did this strength come from? What nurtures strength in even the most wounded among us?

- The author shifted between scenes from her childhood and scenes from her adult life. What did this back-and-forth writing style add to the narrative?

- The author shared extremely personal and painful experiences. Are there experiences in your past that you find too difficult to divulge? Have you every shared a secret from your past that helped you get through it?

- The title of the book is *House of Fire: A story of love, courage, and transformation*. Where did you find these elements in the text?

Resources

Jane A. Hodgdon Rodich, MBA, MA, LMF
JARodichLMFT@gmail.com
EMDR trained therapist. Embraces an eclectic approach to therapy, including collaborative therapy, in whichshe encourages clients to reach conclusions and make decisions for their own lives as a means of empowerment.

Cindy Libman, LICSW, LMFT, CAEH
www.cindylibman.com
Heart-centered therapy.

De Familia a Familia (birthmother search)
www.defamiliaafamilia.com
De Familia a Familia has been for over twenty-five years the link of communication between birth and adoptive families, with the aim of helping them maintain and strengthen a healthy relationship. De Familia facilitates the contact through photographs, letters and personal meetings.

Los Elementos Adventure Center
www.kayakguatemala.com/index.html
Travel in Guatemala.

Loft Literary Center
www.loft.org
One of the nation's leading literary art centers.

WordSisters Blog
www.wordsisters.wordpress.com

Elizabeth di Grazia's Website
www.elizabethdigrazia.com

Acknowledgements

This book has been thirty years in the making. I have many people to thank who have been instrumental in seeing it to print.

First and foremost, Loft Mentor Mark Anthony Rollo. My brother in arms, we spent countless hours around the firepit envisioning *House of Fire*. Like the smoke that rose from the burning wood, his words, his wisdom, permeate these pages. I'll be forever thankful for our time together.

Thank you, Jerald Walker, acclaimed author and mentor, for believing in this memoir.

A huge thanks to Mary Carroll Moore, who breathed life into *House of Fire* with her suggestion that I interweave my past and present and then taught me how to do it.

More thanks to my first MFA Hamline instructor, Judith Katz, who told me that I had the words to say but didn't know how to say it, and to the Hamline instructors who taught me how to say it—Mary Francois Rockcastle, Patricia Weaver Francisco, Deborah Keenan, Barrie Borich, Larry Sutin, Sheila O'Connor, and to Alison McGhee, who is a champion of bravery. A special thanks to Scott Edelstein, who was the first of those instructors and who has continued to offer his guidance and support.

Much gratitude to my mothers in healing: Marie Boehlke, Ruth Markowitz, Wendy Farrar, Cindy Libman, Bea, and Jane Rodich. You held me until I didn't need you and released me to the next when it was time.

A profound thanks to my writer's group of over thirteen years, the many Saturday mornings and the careful readings of *House of Fire* in its many forms. Ellen Shriner—my WordSisters partner—Brenda van Dyck, Jean Cook, Jill Smith, and to Lisa Lake, who has passed on but is not forgotten—a place for her always at our table—and to Rosemary Davis, whose enthusiasm knows no bounds.

Heartfelt thanks to CNF Loft mentees, fellow compatriots Ember Johnson, Pam Schmid, and Welcome Jerde.

My love and deep appreciation to my friend, Sarah Brown.

All of the above wouldn't have happened without the support of the Jerome Travel and Study Grant, Loft Mentor Series, and a Next Step Grant from the McKnight Foundation and the Loft Literary Center, where I first met instructor Deidre Pope many, many years ago and wrote my first poem.

Thank you to the faithful readers of WordSisters; you honor me with your presence.

House of Fire is dedicated to my partner, Jody, whose love and support is constant; Antonio, my *Juan José*; and my daughter Crystel, who will one day be famous.